Pollution

Other Books in the Current Controversies Series

Current
CONTROVERSIES

Pollution

Debra A. Miller, Book Editor

GREENHAVEN PRESS
A part of Gale, Cengage Learning

GALE
CENGAGE Learning·

Detroit • New York • San Francisco • New Haven, Conn • Waterville, Maine • London

Elizabeth Des Chenes, *Managing Editor*

© 2012 Greenhaven Press, a part of Gale, Cengage Learning

Gale and Greenhaven Press are registered trademarks used herein under license.

For more information, contact:
Greenhaven Press
27500 Drake Rd.
Farmington Hills, MI 48331-3535
Or you can visit our Internet site at gale.cengage.com

For product information and technology assistance, contact us at

Gale Customer Support, 1-800-877-4253
For permission to use material from this text or product, submit all requests online at
www.cengage.com/permissions

Further permissions questions can be emailed to permissionrequest@cengage.com

Articles in Greenhaven Press anthologies are often edited for length to meet page requirements. In addition, original titles of these works are changed to clearly present the main thesis and to explicitly indicate the author's opinion. Every effort is made to ensure that Greenhaven Press accurately reflects the original intent of the authors. Every effort has been made to trace the owners of copyrighted material.

Cover image copyright © ssuaphotos/Shutterstock.com.

LIBRARY OF CONGRESS CATALOGING-IN-PUBLICATION DATA

Pollution / Debra A. Miller, book editor.
    p. cm. -- (Current controversies)
    Includes bibliographical references and index.
    ISBN 978-0-7377-5634-0 (hardcover) -- ISBN 978-0-7377-5635-7 (pbk.)
  1. Pollution. I. Miller, Debra A.
  TD174.P923 2012
  363.73--dc23
                                        2011037690

Printed in the United States of America
1 2 3 4 5 6 7 16 15 14 13 12

Contents

US drinking water has improved significantly since 1962 due to the Environmental Protection Agency's requirments to test water daily. US tap water can be as healthy to drink as bottled water and is more environmentally friendly. The debate between bottled water and tap water comes down to taste and convenience issues.

Chapter 2: Is Global Warming a Real Environmental Threat?

Although there will always be some uncertainties in understanding the Earth's complex climate system, a large body of scientific evidence has documented that the global climate is changing, largely because of human activities. Climate change is already affecting us and will pose significant threats to human and natural systems in the future, so more scientific research is needed to allow the world to understand and respond to this phenomenon.

No: Global Warming Is Not a Real Environmental Threat

Chapter 3: Are Environmental Efforts Adequate to Meet Pollution Challenges?

China's new five-year plan, released in March 2011, is the most environmentally ambitious the country has ever announced. It prioritizes curbing greenhouse gases and improving the environment as a key element of China's economic path. China also plans to limit the total amount of energy usage—a goal that will involve dramatic increases in energy efficiency and use of green energy sources, such as hydropower, wind, solar, and nuclear energy.

No: Environmental Efforts Are Not Adequate to Meet Pollution Challenges

The world's biggest companies continue to use natural resources without paying for the damage to the environment—causing $2.2 trillion worth of environmental damage in 2008 alone, according to a study by a London-based consultancy firm. If corporate polluters were forced by governments to pay for the costs of their environmental impact, however, they could lose up to one-third of their profits.

Chapter 4: What Are the Emerging Solutions to Environmental Pollution?

The United States should adopt a Clean Energy Standard (CES)—a mandate for electric utilities to generate a certain percentage of their power from clean energy sources—as a first step in moving the country toward a clean energy economy. This would stimulate demand for clean energy products and allow the United States to catch up to countries such as China and Germany, which currently are leading the world in clean technology.

   VOAnews.com

   Pollution is a global problem so it requires global solutions. The US Environmental Protection Agency (EPA) is committed to combating pollution on an international level, and it plans to take steps such as helping other countries formulate effective environmental regulations, reduce greenhouse gas emissions, improve air and water quality, reduce the chemicals and toxins in food and other consumer products, and address the problem of e-waste.

Foreword

By definition, controversies are "discussions of questions in which opposing opinions clash" (*Webster's Twentieth Century Dictionary Unabridged*). Few would deny that controversies are a pervasive part of the human condition and exist on virtually every level of human enterprise. Controversies transpire between individuals and among groups, within nations and between nations. Controversies supply the grist necessary for progress by providing challenges and challengers to the status quo. They also create atmospheres where strife and warfare can flourish. A world without controversies would be a peaceful world; but it also would be, by and large, static and prosaic.

The Series' Purpose

The purpose of the Current Controversies series is to explore many of the social, political, and economic controversies dominating the national and international scenes today. Titles selected for inclusion in the series are highly focused and specific. For example, from the larger category of criminal justice, Current Controversies deals with specific topics such as police brutality, gun control, white collar crime, and others. The debates in Current Controversies also are presented in a useful, timeless fashion. Articles and book excerpts included in each title are selected if they contribute valuable, long-range ideas to the overall debate. And wherever possible, current information is enhanced with historical documents and other relevant materials. Thus, while individual titles are current in focus, every effort is made to ensure that they will not become quickly outdated. Books in the Current Controversies series will remain important resources for librarians, teachers, and students for many years.

In addition to keeping the titles focused and specific, great care is taken in the editorial format of each book in the series. Book introductions and chapter prefaces are offered to provide background material for readers. Chapters are organized around several key questions that are answered with diverse opinions representing all points on the political spectrum. Materials in each chapter include opinions in which authors clearly disagree as well as alternative opinions in which authors may agree on a broader issue but disagree on the possible solutions. In this way, the content of each volume in Current Controversies mirrors the mosaic of opinions encountered in society. Readers will quickly realize that there are many viable answers to these complex issues. By questioning each author's conclusions, students and casual readers can begin to develop the critical thinking skills so important to evaluating opinionated material.

Current Controversies is also ideal for controlled research. Each anthology in the series is composed of primary sources taken from a wide gamut of informational categories including periodicals, newspapers, books, US and foreign government documents, and the publications of private and public organizations. Readers will find factual support for reports, debates, and research papers covering all areas of important issues. In addition, an annotated table of contents, an index, a book and periodical bibliography, and a list of organizations to contact are included in each book to expedite further research.

Perhaps more than ever before in history, people are confronted with diverse and contradictory information. During the Persian Gulf War, for example, the public was not only treated to minute-to-minute coverage of the war, it was also inundated with critiques of the coverage and countless analyses of the factors motivating US involvement. Being able to sort through the plethora of opinions accompanying today's major issues, and to draw one's own conclusions, can be a complicated and frustrating struggle. It is the editors' hope that Current Controversies will help readers with this struggle.

Introduction

"E-waste is now the fastest growing type
of trash and it is highly hazardous, containing toxic materials such as persistent
organic pollutants and heavy metals."

The word pollution is usually associated with polluted air,
water, and soils, but the proliferation of electronic technology that began with televisions, computers, and cell phones
has produced a new type of pollution called electronic waste,
or e-waste. In fact, e-waste is now the fastest growing type of
trash and it is highly hazardous, containing toxic materials
such as persistent organic pollutants and heavy metals.

The e-waste problem is significant partly because experts
see no end in sight. More and more consumers are buying
new electronic gadgets at an alarming rate, as their old electronics stop working or quickly become obsolete. Manufacturers encourage these sales by producing cheap products that
are not made to last and by continually introducing new technological products that make the old versions seem less desir-
able. Apple, for example, is known for its success in marketing
new iPhones, iPads, and other products every few months.
Similarly, cell phone companies offer customers cell phone
upgrades for free or at discounted prices if they sign new service contracts. And in 2009, television broadcasters in the
United States switched from an analog to digital TV signal—a
decision that caused millions of people to throw out their
older televisions and purchase new high-definition TVs (even
though the old TVs would still work with a converter box).

This trend of throw-away electronics is creating a mountain of e-waste around the world. The United States alone
produces about four hundred million pieces of electronic
trash each year, and globally between twenty and fifty million

tons of e-waste is created annually. The rapid rise of emerging economies in the developing world, such as India and China, is compounding the e-waste problem, because millions of new consumers are demanding the same kinds of technology as people in the developed countries.

The main issue with e-waste, however, is that electronic products contain very toxic materials. According to the Electronics TakeBack Coalition, a group that promotes green design and responsible recycling of electronics, more than one thousand types of toxic materials—including heavy metals, plastics, gases, chlorinated solvents, and brominated flame retardants—are used to make electronic products and components, such as computer disc drives, circuit boards, and semiconductor chips. Computer monitors, the group reports, can contain between four and eight pounds of lead. Big screen TVs, meanwhile, also contain large amounts of lead, and flat screen TVs use mercury lamps. Heavy metals such as lead, mercury, and cadmium are known health hazards. Lead causes brain damage in children; cadmium destroys the kidneys; and mercury causes both brain and kidney damage, even at extremely low dosages. Allowing these and other toxins into the human food or water supply, experts say, is a recipe for disaster.

Yet much of this e-waste—some estimates say more than 80 percent—ends up in landfills, where it can leach toxins into the soil and water supply, or incinerators, where burning of plastics can produce dioxin, yet another toxin. The rest of the e-waste is recycled. However, many recycling companies located in developed countries like the United States do not recycle the e-waste themselves. Instead, they export the electronics to developing countries such as China, where the lack of health and safety laws allow crude recycling methods that release toxins into the air and surrounding soils. In many cases, this means that poor people dismantle old TVs and computers in the open air using hammers and fire without any type of protections, exposing themselves and their families repeatedly to poisons that can be very damaging to human health. These poor recyclers then sell some of the retrieved metals, but other unwanted plastics, glass, and toxins are often discarded into dumps or rivers, causing more pollution.

In fact, a study published in May 2011 found that pollutants from e-waste accumulate in the human body and cause damage to lung cells, increasing the risk of a number of diseases, including cancer and heart disease. Researchers in this study selected one of the largest e-waste recycling regions in China and took lung cell samples from people at two sites located downwind from the recycling center. The lung cells were tested for two markers—Interleukin-8 (IL-8), which indicates inflammatory response, and reactive oxygen species (ROS), which can cause stress in lungs—as well as for a gene (p53) that is triggered if cell damage is taking place. The results showed that e-waste pollutants caused significant increases in both IL-8 and ROS levels, as well as increases in the p53 gene. The study's authors concluded that these changes indicate DNA damage in the lung that could lead to serious disease for those affected.

Environmental advocates say the answer to the e-waste problem is two-fold. First, companies must produce electronic products that are safer and last longer, and second, electronics manufacturers must be held responsible for their products from cradle-to-grave—that is, they must take back their products and responsibly recycle them at the end of the product lifespan. In the United States, there is no national law requiring this type of manufacturer responsibility, but twenty-five states have now enacted producer responsibility laws.

The e-waste issue demonstrates that the fight against pollution is an important and never-ending struggle. Even as solutions are developed for some types of pollution, human activities inevitably produce other types of pollution problems—a pattern that requires constant vigilance. The authors of the viewpoints in *Current Controversies: Pollution* discuss other forms of pollution, such as air pollution, water pollution, and the carbon pollution that experts say is causing global warming. Issues debated include whether air and water pollution continue to be serious environmental problems, whether global warming is a real environmental threat, whether environmental efforts are adequate to address the world's environmental problems, and what are some of the emerging solutions to today's pollution.

CHAPTER 1

Are Air and Water Pollution Serious Environmental Problems?

Chapter Preface

A lthough air pollution is frequently thought of as a problem with pollutants in outdoor air, indoor air can be an
even bigger threat to human health. According to the US Environmental Protection Agency (EPA), indoor air may contain
two to five times as many pollutants as outdoor air. High levels of indoor air pollution are particularly worrisome because
most people spend large portions of their time indoors—
working, relaxing, and sleeping.

The sources of indoor air pollution are varied. Cigarette
smoke is one of the most common indoor pollutants, affecting both smokers and nonsmokers who are exposed to the
smoking environment. This secondhand smoke causes cancer,
respiratory infections, sudden infant death syndrome, and
asthma, and despite recent antismoking efforts, it still accounts for nearly fifty thousand deaths per year in the United
States. Other sources of combustion, such as stoves, furnaces,
fireplaces, heaters, and clothes dryers, can also produce indoor
toxins, including carbon monoxide—a colorless, odorless gas
that can be fatal. Carbon monoxide fatalities—up to four
hundred fifty US deaths per year—occur most frequently during the winter months, when heating devices malfunction or
are improperly used.

Houses themselves can also contain unhealthy substances.
Sometimes, homes are built on soils that contain radon—a
colorless, odorless, radioactive gas caused by the natural break-
down of uranium. The gas seeps into homes and unless de-
tected can cause lung cancer. According to the EPA, radon is
responsible for up to thirty thousand lung cancer deaths per
year in the United States.

Other indoor toxins are contained in building materials,
furniture, and various products used in the home, such as
paints, cleaning supplies, and pesticides. One category of pol-

lutants is called volatile organic compounds (VOCs) and includes a host of dangerous chemicals, such as benzene, formaldehyde, chloroform, and toluene. Some of these VOCs, like formaldehyde, are known to cause cancer. Many older homes and buildings, meanwhile, pose the threat of poisoning from lead, a metal that causes brain damage in children and problems with kidneys, nerves, or blood pressure in adults. This is because in years past lead was widely used in paints, caulking, and other building products. Yet another dangerous building material is asbestos, a type of mineral once widely used in insulation, roof shingles, heating systems, and flooring. When asbestos is disturbed, tiny microscopic fibers are released into the air, and inhalation of these fibers increases the risk of lung cancer and mesothelioma, a cancer that attacks the lining around the lungs and other organs.

The safety of indoor air also can be compromised by a variety of irritants that can cause asthma or other diseases. One of the most common indoor allergens is dust mites, microscopic insects that live in household dust and feed on discarded human skin cells. Almost all homes have some level of this pollutant, frequently found in bedding or upholstery. Other insects, such as cockroaches, pose a similar danger of asthma and allergies. Another very common indoor allergen comes from pet dander, flecks of skin shed by furry or feathered animals. Houses, too, can become fertile ground for the growth of biological pollutants such as mold, bacteria, and viruses—all a source of tiny particles that can become airborne, be inhaled by people living in the home, and produce infections and diseases in humans. Mold is one of the most dangerous problems; it grows anywhere there is high humidity or dampness, and produces spores that float throughout the house and can cause everything from colds to chronic illness.

People in the developing world have even more to worry about from indoor air pollution. In these poorer countries, many people still cook on open fires or wood-fired cookstoves, and these can repeatedly expose people to smoke that can cause serious health problems, including bronchitis, childhood pneumonia, emphysema, lung cancer, and heart disease. In fact, some estimates say that up to three billion people in the developing world are regularly exposed to cookstove smoke and that it causes almost two million premature deaths each year.

The key solution for the problem of indoor air pollution, in many cases, is simple awareness. In developed countries, tests are available for pollutants such as radon, carbon dioxide, mold, and other pollutants, and homeowners can reduce indoor air pollution by more carefully selecting the products they buy and use in the home. In the developing world, advocates say that cleaner and more efficient cookstoves and proper ventilation with chimneys or open windows would significantly reduce pollution levels. By comparison, the problems of outdoor air and water pollution require more difficult and costly fixes. The United States and other countries have made concerted efforts to address these types of pollution, and the viewpoints in this chapter debate the question of whether air and water pollution continue to be serious environmental problems.

Carbon Dioxide Pollution from Power Plants Rose in the United States in 2010

The Environmental Integrity Project

The Environmental Integrity Project, a nonprofit organization founded by former Environmental Protection Agency (EPA) attorneys, advocates for more effective enforcement of environmental laws and regulations.

Carbon dioxide emissions from power plants rose 5.56% in 2010 over the year before, the biggest annual increase since the Environmental Protection Agency [EPA] began tracking emissions in 1995. Electricity generators released 2.423 billion tons of carbon dioxide (CO_2) in 2010, compared to 2.295 billion tons in 2009, according to information available on EPA's "Clean Air Markets" database. While the increase is worrisome, power plant emissions are still below the high water mark of 2.565 billion tons set in 2007. Last year's rise was driven in part by a 3.0% net increase in overall generation for the 12 months ending in November of 2010, due to the economic recovery and unusually warm weather in some parts of the country.

Average global temperatures last year reached the 2005 level, the warmest year on record. CO_2 is the most prevalent of the greenhouse gases that cause global warming; the combustion of fossil fuels for electricity generation in the U.S. accounts for more than one third of our nation's total U.S. releases of CO_2, and more than nearly 5% of CO_2 emissions worldwide. Coal-fired boilers provided 45% of our electricity in 2010, but were responsible for 81% of total U.S. CO_2 emissions from electricity generation last year.

"Getting Warmer: US CO_2 Emissions from Power Plants Emissions Rise 5.6% in 2010," The Environmental Integrity Project, February 18, 2011. Used by permission.

Coal the Biggest Polluter

Texas power plants led the pack in 2010, with nearly 257 million tons of CO_2 emissions, as much as the next two states combined (Florida and Ohio), and more than 7 times the total CO_2 emissions from power plants in California. Despite a favorable climate for wind energy and falling natural gas prices, Texas opened three new coal plants toward the end of 2010, with a combined capacity of 2,156 megawatts. . . .

Fifty coal-fired power plants accounted for 750 million tons of CO_2 emissions in 2010, or about a third of the total. The two largest carbon polluters, the Scherer and Bowen power plants in Georgia, together released more than 48 million tons of CO_2 in 2010. By comparison, emissions from all power plants in California were 37.1 million tons; in New York, 40.0 million tons; and in the six states of New England, 40.5 million tons.

> *The Clean Air Act and other environmental laws, falling natural gas prices, and the growing market for renewable energy could curb greenhouse gas emissions from coal-fired plants.*

Coal-fired generation rose 5.2% in the 12 months ending November 30, 2010, growing at a faster pace than the overall 3.0% increase in net generation over the same period. But net generation of wind powered electricity, although a much smaller fraction of total output, rose from 73.6 to 92.7 million megawatts, for a 26% increase through the end of November last year. Net generation from natural gas fired plants, which release less than half as much carbon dioxide as coal plants on a per megawatt basis, rose 6.8% over the same period.

Sulfur dioxide (SO_2) emissions from power plants decreased from 5.72 million to 5.11 million tons between 2009 and 2010, while nitrogen oxide (NO_x) emissions increased slightly over the same time span. Emissions of both pollutants have declined more than 50% over the past ten years, though progress is uneven. For example, sulfur dioxide has actually increased slightly in Missouri, while declining more than 85% in Maryland. The overall trend is encouraging and emissions of SO_2 and NOx should decline still further, unless the Republican House majority succeeds in derailing emission standards that are scheduled to take effect within the next four years. . . .

Curbing Coal Emissions

Congress has declined to pass comprehensive legislation to address global warming. But the Clean Air Act and other environmental laws, falling natural gas prices, and the growing market for renewable energy could curb greenhouse gas emissions from coal-fired plants. Most of the more than one hundred proposals to build new coal plants that surfaced several years ago have been withdrawn, having been defeated by local opposition, legal challenges, and the erosion of marketplace advantages that coal-fired power used to enjoy.

Nearly 4.5 gigawatts of new coal-fired electric generation came on line in 2010, about half of that in Texas. But power companies have also announced plans to retire almost 12 gigawatts of coal-fired capacity within the next few years, including the announcement last month that Xcel would close nearly 900 megawatts of coal-fired capacity at four different power stations in Colorado. More announcements are expected this year, as companies wisely choose to shut down aging boilers, rather than pay to retrofit dirty and outdated plants to comply with federal air, waste and water standards.

These new rules include regulations requiring the cleanup of mercury and other toxic pollutants from power plants, additional reductions of sulfur dioxide and nitrogen oxide at plants that do not already have state-of-the-art controls, and potential new standards for ash disposal that will require closure of leaking ash ponds used to dispose of the industry's waste. This summer [2011], the EPA will propose standards to limit CO_2 emissions from power plants under the Clean Air Act, in the wake of a 2007 Supreme Court decision finding that greenhouse gases were pollutants subject to regulation under the act. By law, any standard that EPA proposes must be affordable and technologically feasible, but even modest limits on CO_2 pollution would at least slow down the buildup of carbon in the earth's atmosphere.

The phase out of the worst polluters would make room for cleaner technologies, like the 3.6 gigawatts of wind power installed in 2010, which could add momentum to the economic recovery while reducing global warming and damage to the public's health from dirty coal plants.

The industry's allies on Capitol Hill [Washington, DC] are working hard to turn back the clock by repealing environmental standards for coal plants that are already many years overdue. Congress may weaken or even eliminate EPA's ability to stop coal plant pollution, and block further study of climate change. But even the most powerful legislature in the world is subject to the laws of science, and global warming will not disappear because our politicians choose to pretend it does not exist.

Industrial Agriculture Is Causing Substantial Water Pollution in the United States

Sustainable Table

Sustainable Table is an ongoing project and related website, created in 2003 by the nonprofit organization GRACE, to help consumers understand problems associated with industrial farming and to educate them about the need for a more sustainable food production system.

Industrial agriculture is one of the leading causes of water pollution in the United States today. In the 2000 National Water Quality Inventory conducted by the Environmental Protection Agency (EPA), agricultural activity was identified as a source of pollution for 48% of stream and river water, and for 41% of lake water.

Water pollution from industrial farms not only damages the environment and kills wildlife, but it can also sicken and kill people. And since these farms exercise little restraint when it comes to water usage, they tend to waste large quantities of water, even when neighboring communities are experiencing water shortages. Because small, sustainable farms are more integrated with their surrounding communities, they pay closer attention to the ways that they use water and how their practices affect local water supplies.

Sources of Pollutants

Most water pollution from industrial farms results from the storage and disposal of animal waste. Industrial livestock farms store manure and other farm wastes in gigantic tanks known as "lagoons" which can hold millions of gallons of manure and urine. Unfortunately, these lagoons often leak and—during large storms—they may rupture or simply overflow. When this happens, the environmental damage can be devastating, as raw manure is up to 160 times more toxic than raw municipal sewage. Leaking lagoons also release antibiotic residues and harmful bacteria that can leach into water supplies.

Many of the pollutants produced by farms (minerals, chemicals and pathogens, to name a few) can make water unsafe for human consumption.

In order to dispose of manure after it's been stored in lagoons, industrial farms spray the waste onto farm fields as fertilizer. Unfortunately, these farms produce far more waste than can be applied to fields, and once the saturation point has been reached, the waste runs off into nearby water systems. The most common form of water pollution in the United States is excess levels of nitrogen or phosphorous, both of which are largely caused by fertilizer runoff. When manure is spread on fields as a fertilizer, it can also introduce some of the more toxic substances present in livestock excretions, such as pharmaceuticals or bacteria. Water pollution from manure as well as synthetic fertilizers can lead to serious environmental damage and harm human health.

Types and Effects of Pollutants

Agricultural water pollution can have variety of negative effects. Not only do substantial environmental problems result, but many of the pollutants produced by farms (minerals, chemicals and pathogens, to name a few) can make water unsafe for human consumption.

Nutrients

Nutrients, such as nitrogen and phosphorous, are the minerals in fertilizer that promote plant growth. But due to the over-fertilization of cropland, far more nitrogen and phosphorous are applied to fields than are removed by crops. Excess nutrients in water cause harmful plant growth—commonly referred to as "algal bloom," which can cause fish kills.

Ammonia and Nitrates

Livestock manure is high in ammonia concentrations, and dissolved ammonia in water is not only highly toxic to fish, but can also be converted to dangerous nitrates. Elevated nitrate levels in drinking water are highly poisonous to humans, causing potentially fatal oxygen levels in babies (known as "blue-baby syndrome"), spontaneous abortions, and possibly cancer: in a sample of wells surveyed by the US Geological Survey from 1993 to 2000, 2 percent of public-supply and 9 percent of the domestic wells more common in rural areas were found to have nitrate concentrations higher than the EPA's maximum allowable level. The EPA estimates that about 1.3 million households in counties with industrial livestock facilities get their water from wells with dangerously high nitrate levels.

Pathogens and Other Microorganisms

Manure contains a high level of pathogens (disease-causing microorganisms). When the waste is applied to fields, those pathogens can be transferred to local water supplies during a run off from either irrigation or rainfall. The impact of pathogens from manure is severe: according to the Centers for Disease Control, in every waterborne disease outbreak in the United States from 1986 to 1998 where the pathogen could be identified, it most likely originated in livestock.

Some other waterborne microorganisms do not originate on farms, but develop as a result of eutrophication caused by high nutrient levels. *Pfiesteria piscicida*, for example, thrives in many areas where algal blooms grow, and causes lesions in fish and large-scale fish kills. It can also cause a range of symptoms in humans, including respiratory and eye irritation, gastrointestinal problems, fatigue, as well as skin problems and cognitive symptoms such as memory loss and confusion.

Antibiotics and Hormones

Antibiotic and artificial growth hormones are commonly used on industrial farms, either injected directly into the livestock or added to their feed. Large amounts of both substances end up being excreted by animals and can thus pollute water along with everything else in livestock waste. Some hormones can remain functional in manure up to 270 days after excretion, and there have been many documented cases of hormones discovered miles downstream of farms. Although it is unclear whether these hormone concentrations can be high enough to affect humans, they have been shown to compromise the reproductive processes of fish.

An estimated 75% of all antibiotics administered to livestock are excreted, and for certain common antibiotics that figure can be as high as 90%. The overuse of antibiotics for livestock contributes to the development of antimicrobial-resistant bacteria, and some studies suggest that growth of these resistant bacteria may be promoted in waterways with high levels of antibiotics. Numerous studies have demonstrated that waterways are a prominent means of transmitting these dangerous types of bacteria to humans.

Heavy Metals and Salts

Some heavy metals, such as copper and zinc, are essential nutrients for animal growth—especially for cattle, swine, and poultry. However, such elements are often present in animal feed in concentrations far higher than necessary for animal health, along with other heavy metals such as chromium, lead, arsenic and cadmium. Farm animals excrete excess heavy metals in their manure—which in turn gets spread as fertilizer, leading to soil and water pollution. The health hazards resulting from exposure to heavy metals in water include kidney problems from cadmium; nervous system disorders, kidney problems and headaches from lead; and both cardiovascular and nervous system problems from arsenic, which is also known to cause cancer.

Many salts are also present in large quantities in manure, including sodium, calcium magnesium, potassium, chloride, sulfate, bicarbonate, carbonate, and nitrate. When introduced to the environment, these salts increase the salinity of waterways, leading to changes in aquatic ecosystems and making water brackish, and therefore unfit for drinking.

Agriculture uses a staggering amount of water on an annual basis.

Organic Matter and Other Solids

In addition to the biodegradable organic matter naturally present in manure, animal bedding, wasted feed, soil, dust, hair and feathers are often mixed with manure in storage and can end up in waterways. The decomposition of organic matter can cause increased levels of bacteria, which in turn reduces oxygen levels in water and kills fish. This decomposition can also negatively affect the color, taste, and smell of water.

Water Usage and Conservation

Agriculture uses a staggering amount of water on an annual basis. In 2000, 41% of all freshwater used by humans in the United States was used for agriculture. Perhaps even more notable is that agriculture accounted for more than 80% of US "consumptive use" of water—that share of water which is not returned quickly to the environment.

Water overuse is particularly a problem on industrial farms that do not tailor their farming practices on a case by case basis. For example, a dairy that uses an automatic "flushing" system to clean out its animal houses uses an average of 150 gallons of water per cow per day, compared to an average of 5-10 gallons used by farms that monitor their water use in order to conserve it. Not only does water overuse hurt the environment, it's also expensive. One estimate from the USDA [US Department of Agriculture] concludes that increasing water use efficiency on irrigated farms by just 10% could save almost $200 million per year solely due to the associated savings in fuel costs.

What You Can Do

Small, sustainable farms conserve water and apply waste and fertilizer to fields responsibly, minimizing their impact on local water systems. By supporting small farms such as these, you can help to promote healthier waterways while showing that you do not support the environmental recklessness practiced by industrial farms.

Ocean Pollution
Is a Global Threat

WWF

WWF is an independent international conservation organization that seeks to stop the degradation of the planet's natural environment.

A staggering amount of waste—much of which has only existed for the past 60 years or so—enters the oceans each year. Over 80% of marine pollution comes from land-based activities.

From plastic bags to pesticides—most of the waste we produce on land eventually reaches the oceans, either through deliberate dumping or from run-off through drains and rivers. This includes:

Oil Spills

Oil spills cause huge damage to the marine environment—but in fact are responsible for only around 12% of the oil entering the seas each year. According to a study by the US National Research Council, 36% comes down drains and rivers as waste and runoff from cities and industry.

Fertilizers

Fertilizer runoff from farms and lawns is a huge problem for coastal areas. The extra nutrients cause eutrophication—flourishing of algal blooms that deplete the water's dissolved oxygen and suffocate other marine life.

Eutrophication has created enormous dead zones in several parts of the world, including the Gulf of Mexico and the Baltic Sea

"Marine Problems: Pollution," WWF. Used by permission of WWF.

Seas of Garbage

Solid garbage also makes its way to the ocean. Plastic bags, balloons, glass bottles, shoes, packaging material—if not disposed of correctly, almost everything we throw away can reach the sea.

Plastic garbage, which decomposes very slowly, is often mistaken for food by marine animals. High concentrations of plastic material, particularly plastic bags, have been found blocking the breathing passages and stomachs of many marine species, including whales, dolphins, seals, puffins, and turtles. Plastic six-pack rings for drink bottles can also choke marine animals.

This garbage can also come back to shore, where it pollutes beaches and other coastal habitats.

Sewage Disposal

In many parts of the world, sewage flows untreated, or under-treated, into the ocean. For example, 80% of urban sewage discharged into the Mediterranean Sea is untreated.

This sewage can also lead to eutrophication. In addition, it can cause human disease and lead to beach closures.

Toxic Chemicals

Almost every marine organism, from the tiniest plankton to whales and polar bears, is contaminated with man-made chemicals, such as pesticides and chemicals used in common consumer products.

Some of these chemicals enter the sea through deliberate dumping. For centuries, the oceans have been a convenient dumping ground for waste generated on land. This continued until the 1970s, with dumping at sea the accepted practise for disposal of nearly everything, including toxic material such as pesticides, chemical weapons, and radioactive waste.

Dumping of the most toxic materials was banned by the London Dumping Convention in 1972, and an amended treaty in 1996 (the London Convention) further restricted what could be dumped at sea. However, there are still the problems of already-dumped toxic material, and even the disposal of permitted substances at sea can be a substantial environmental hazard.

People once assumed that the ocean was so large that all pollutants would be diluted and dispersed to safe levels. But in reality, they have not disappeared.

Chemicals also enter the sea from land-based activities. Chemicals can escape into water, soil, and air during their manufacture, use, or disposal, as well as from accidental leaks or fires in products containing these chemicals. Once in the environment, they can travel for long distances in air and water, including ocean currents.

People once assumed that the ocean was so large that all pollutants would be diluted and dispersed to safe levels. But in reality, they have not disappeared—and some toxic man-made chemicals have even become more concentrated as they have entered the food chain.

Tiny animals at the bottom of the food chain, such as plankton in the oceans, absorb the chemicals as they feed. Because they do not break down easily, the chemicals accumulate in these organisms, becoming much more concentrated in their bodies than in the surrounding water or soil. These organisms are eaten by small animals, and the concentration rises again. These animals are in turn eaten by larger animals, which can travel large distances with their even further increased chemical load.

Animals higher up the food chain, such as seals, can have contamination levels millions of times higher than the water in which they live. And polar bears, which feed on seals, can have contamination levels up to 3 billion times higher than their environment.

People become contaminated either directly from household products or by eating contaminated seafood and animal fats.

Evidence is mounting that a number of man-made chemicals can cause serious health problems—including cancer, damage to the immune system, behavioural problems, and reduced fertility.

China's Economic Development Has Caused Serious Global Pollution Issues

Ty Butler

Ty Butler is a master of international affairs candidate at the School of International Affairs at Pennsylvania State University.

Over the past decade China's economy has boomed. Growing at an almost unfathomable rate, China's recent economic growth has been beyond impressive reaching upwards of over 11% per year (11.4% in 2007).[1] The growth has helped to lift millions out of poverty and has thrust China into the global spotlight making it the second largest economy in the world. This success though carries with it potentially crippling costs for China; costs which up until now, have been glossed over or given minimal real attention and which are starting to take its toll as the country's GDP [gross domestic product, a measure of a country's total economic output] growth for 2011 is expected (at 7%) to be at its lowest level since 1999.[2]

A growth rate of 7% is still impressive even if it is below the 8% that Chinese authorities were aiming to keep it at, but is even a 7% growth rate sustainable for China? As China has grown, it has relied on rather dirty industry to propel it economically. This, coupled with a heavy reliance on coal as an energy source along with rapid urbanization trends and soaring car usage have devastated the Chinese environment and its ability to absorb the effects of future growth.

1. "GDP growth in China 1952–2009." *Chinability*. http://www.chinability.com/GDP.htm.

2. "China pollution 'threatens growth.'" BBC News. 28 Feb. 2011. http://www.bbc.co.uk /news/world-asia-pacific-12595872.

Ty Butler, "The Cost of Growth: Pollution Externalities in China," Penn State Global Forum, April 12, 2011. Used by permission of the author.

China's Pollution

China has become the highest producer of both sulfur dioxide and CO_2 [carbon dioxide] pollution in the world, choking its cities with smog and poor air quality that contain particle levels well above average western safety rates. The poor air quality, according to a World Bank study has made China home to 16 of the top 20 most polluted cities in the world.[3] Only 1 percent of the country's 560 million urban citizens have access to air that is considered safe to breathe by European Union standards.[4]

> Air pollution from China has caused acid rain to fall on its neighbors such as Japan and South Korea, ... [and even] the United States feels the impact of Chinese [air] pollution.

Acid rain, caused by high levels of sulfur dioxide emissions, falls on 1/4th of the entire country and on a full 1/3rd of Chinese agricultural land.[5] Acid rain has likewise become a significant problem for China's cities as well, affecting approximately 200 out of the 440 cities that the Chinese government monitored for a 2010 report.[6]

Air pollution levels have become so high that it has even started to cause shifts in weather patterns over China leading

3. Lagorio, Christine. "The Most Polluted Places On Earth." CBS News. 8 Jan. 2010. http://www.cbsnews.com/stories/2007/06/06/eveningnews/main2895653.shtml.

4. Kahn, Joseph, and Jim Yardley. "As China Roars, Pollution Reaches Deadly Extremes." *New York Times.* 26 Aug. 2007. http://www.nytimes.com/2007/08/26/world/asia /26china.html?pagewanted=print.

5. Economy, Elizabeth C. "The Great Leap Backward?" *Foreign Affairs.* Council on Foreign Relations, Oct. 2007. http://www.foreignaffairs.com/articles/62827/elizabeth-c -economy/the-great-leap-backward.

6. Jacobs, Andrew. "In China, Pollution Worsens Despite New Efforts." *New York Times.* 28 July 2010. http://www.nytimes.com/2010/07/29/world/asia/29china.html.

to a 30% decrease in rainfall in almost half of its major river regions as well as a 37% decline in the country's wheat, rice and corn yields. Such drought effects brought on by air pollution coupled with heavy land and water depletion have also led to huge leaps in desertification. The Gobi Desert in northern China is currently expanding by about 1,900 square miles annually (an area twice the size of Luxembourg). All told, somewhere between 1/5th–1/4th of the entire country is now officially classified as desert.[7]

Such desertification and air pollution effects are not hampered by China's borders either. Air pollution from China has caused acid rain to fall on its neighbors such as Japan and South Korea, while the expanding Gobi Desert eats up land at a frightening pace in Mongolia. Even the United States feels the impact of Chinese pollution, most notably in California which is home to some of the most polluted cities in the US. Air pollution from China has had an especially heavy impact on the United States' most polluted city Los Angeles, where roughly 25% of the airborne particulates hail from China.[8]

China's air quality is not the county's only concern. The industrialization process as well as its agricultural practices have severely impacted China's water supplies and soil quality too. The Chinese government declared in 2010 that over 25% of its fresh water systems (rivers, lakes, etc.) were contaminated to the point of being beyond safe for both human consumption and agricultural use, with 70% of China's fresh water being polluted in general.[9] High levels of water usage to sustain China's agricultural sectors coupled with severe pollution, has left China in the midst of a water crisis. Two-thirds

7. Economy, Elizabeth C. "The Great Leap Backward?" *Foreign Affairs.* Council on Foreign Relations, Oct. 2007. http://www.foreignaffairs.com/articles/62827/elizabeth-c-economy/the-great-leap-backward.

8. Lorenz, Andreas, and Wieland Wagner. "China's boom and doom." *Salon.* 12 Feb. 2007. http://www.salon.com/news/feature/2007/02/12/china_pollution/index.html.

9. http://www.worldwatch.org.

of China's cities have less water than is required for basic daily needs and 1/6th of them suffer from severe water shortages. Even those cities with adequate water supplies are burdened by the strain as aquifers in 90% of Chinese cities are polluted and 75% of fresh water ground flows are considered unsafe for consumption (consumption including both drinking and fishing activities).[10]

In rural areas, this water contamination seeps into agricultural land resulting in 10% of China's farmland being dangerously polluted. Overall, every year upwards of 12 million tons of grain in China are contaminated with heavy metals from the soil. Along the coast, water pollution translates into a weakening fishing industry with 80% of the East China Sea currently rated unsuitable for fishing.[11]

Despite the overwhelming scope of China's environmental problems, the central government has been either unable or unwilling to appropriately implement effective reforms.

Health Effects

The effects of Chinese pollution externalities also have had a huge impact on China's most abundant and most important resource: its citizens. It would be hard to overstate the grimness of the human cost of China's development. Pollution within China has caused increased problems with bladder and respiratory health. Contaminated water supplies have become a leading cause of death for children under the age of five as 700 million people in China drink contaminated water on a

10. Economy, Elizabeth C. "The Great Leap Backward?" *Foreign Affairs.* Council on Foreign Relations, Oct. 2007. http://www.foreignaffairs.com/articles/62827/elizabeth-c -economy/the-great-leap-backward.

11. Economy, Elizabeth. "Toxic cost of China's success." *The Sunday Times.* 11 Nov. 2007. http://www.timesonline.co.uk/tol/news/world/asia/article2846875.ece.

daily basis resulting in 190 million Chinese citizens suffering illnesses resulting from contaminated water consumption at any given moment.[12] Such consumption has also witnessed sharp increases in cancer rates (particularly gastrointestinal cancer). Between 2005 and 2007 alone, cancer rates increased by 19% in urban areas and by a staggering 23% in rural areas.[13]

The World Bank, in conjunction with China's own State Environmental Protection Agency has found that China faces 750,000 deaths every year due to the effects of pollution; numbers which have been confirmed by the World Health Organization.[14] This makes pollution one of the leading causes of death within China. So shocking were the numbers that the Chinese government banned domestic publication of the statistics and lobbied the World Bank to exclude them from its report.

China More Concerned with Economy than Environment

Despite the overwhelming scope of China's environmental problems, the central government has been either unable or unwilling to appropriately implement effective reforms. Just this year, China has announced the inclusion of both nitrogen oxide and ammonia nitrogen in its efforts to reduce emissions which it seeks to cut by 1.5% throughout the course of 2011.[15]

12. "China faces severe water crisis." *The Council of Canadians*. 17 Feb. 2011. http://www.canadians.org/campaignblog/?p=6464.

13. Economy, Elizabeth. "Toxic cost of China's success." *The Sunday Times*. 11 Nov. 2007. http://www.timesonline.co.uk/tol/news/world/asia/article2846875.ece.

14. "The Cost of Pollution in China." *World Bank*. Feb. 2007. http://siteresources.worldbank.org/INTEAPREGTOPENVIRONMENT/Resources/China_Cost_of_Pollution.pdf.

15. Watts, Jonathan. "China sets new pollution controls." *Guardian*. 14 Jan. 2011. http://www.guardian.co.uk/environment/2011/jan/14/china-pollution-controls.

A welcome shift in official policy for sure, but will it be carried out? China's recent history is wrought with failed attempts to address environmental problems. In 2004 Hu Jintao, China's current president, announced a new campaign that would list statistics for a Green GDP (one that would take into account the environmental costs associated with economic growth). The program was a fiasco. It was executed well, but the results were so sobering (indicating a revised growth rate of virtually zero for some regions) that the project was scrapped after its first report.[16]

This attitude towards China's pollution problem seems indicative of a government that is strongly concerned with its own image and perhaps one that is worried that low or significantly slowing growth rates may create legitimacy concerns and threaten "social stability." Indeed, across China short run economic progress often takes precedence over environmental considerations, even when said considerations are codified through law. The central government has introduced some decent regulation guidelines to address the worsening environmental situation. Many regulations though seem useful only in PR [public relations] campaigns as they are more often than not completely ignored by regional officials who operate under a central government that doesn't seem overly interested in enforcing its own laws. Only 23% of Chinese factories properly treat their sewage before dumping it and as of 2007 only 10% of China's environmental laws overall are actually enforced.[17]

Even when serious efforts are made to clean areas up, such efforts still fall short. This was clearly the case in Beijing when, in anticipation of hosting the 2008 Summer Olympics,

16. Liu, Melinda. "Where Poor Is A Poor Excuse." *The Daily Beast.* 28 June 2008. http://www.thedailybeast.com/newsweek/2008/06/28/where-poor-is-a-poor-excuse.html.

17. Economy, Elizabeth C. "The Great Leap Backward?" *Foreign Affairs.* Council on Foreign Relations, Oct. 2007. http://www.foreignaffairs.com/articles/62827/elizabeth-c-economy/the-great-leap-backward.

China put forth an enormous effort to clean up a city that contained air pollution rates that were over three times the cutoff level for what is considered safe in Europe. China forced polluting businesses to relocate and placed strict regulations on polluting within the city. These efforts though, were offset by other factors and at the end of 2008 the city still violated the World Health Organization's safety standards roughly 80% of the time.[18] Even by 2010, the city remains in much the same condition as it was before as car ownership within China has soared.

Even China's success stories in the area of environmental reform may be suspect as Chinese government data has been found to have understated the severity of many of China's environmental woes. In 2010, a report was released that showed that China's water pollution problem for example was twice as bad as the government initially claimed it was in 2007. Whether such "mistakes" were intentional or merely the product of poor/half hearted data collection is unclear, but what is clear is that initial claims of success such as in the meeting of 2005 reduction targets for things like chemical oxygen demand (dealing with water pollution) practically remained true only when the faulty data was used.[19]

A Need for Sustainable Development

So what is to be done? The answer seems clear if not, in the central government's opinion, politically viable. China needs to stop sacrificing long run growth and economic sustainability for the sake of short run political and economic gains. China has some decent protection laws, but it needs to find the political motivation and willingness to actually enforce

18. "In China, Pollution Worsens Despite New Efforts." *China Digital Times*. 28 July 2010. http://chinadigitaltimes.net/2010/07/in-china-pollution-worsens-despite-new -efforts.

19. Ansfield, Jonathan, and Keith Bradsher. "China Report Shows More Pollution in Waterways." *New York Times*. 9 Feb. 2010. http://www.nytimes.com/2010/02/10/world /asia/10pollute.html.

them and hold regional administrators accountable for their implementation. If such efforts are not made, then any initiative for combating environmental degradation, no matter how good they appear on paper, are going to fall short in practice.

There are other areas that China can improve in as well. Simple efficiency gains within China's existing and future infrastructure have the potential to make a world of difference. Currently, China often sacrifices efficiency for the sake of speed, a combination which, once again, brings short run gains at the cost of longer run problems. A clear example rests within China's energy sector. China relies primarily on coal for its energy and every year it burns more than the United States, Japan and all of Europe combined. Despite the fact that coal-fired power plants tend to be a very dirty way to generate power, China's are especially dirty as they are generally hastily constructed using low quality methods which result in efficiency losses. Even outside of the low quality of most of these power plants, there exists the prevalence of a multitude of illegal power plants. By the central government's own estimation 20% of China's power plants operate outside of the law.[20]

Efficiency problems affect other areas of the economy as well. China uses 10–20% more water than the US does to irrigate its crops with an additional 20% of water being lost due to poor piping infrastructure (once again a quality issue).[21] China's steel industry uses 25% more energy per ton produced than the international average with the cement industry using 45% more.[22] Even the average building in China faces

20. Jubak, Jim. "How long can China pollute for free?" MSN News. 9 Feb. 2007. http://articles.moneycentral.msn.com/Investing/JubaksJournal/HowLongCanChinaPolluteForFree.aspx.

21. Economy, Elizabeth C. "The Great Leap Backward?" *Foreign Affairs.* Council on Foreign Relations, Oct. 2007. http://www.foreignaffairs.com/articles/62827/elizabeth-c-economy/the-great-leap-backward.

22. Kahn, Joseph, and Jim Yardley. "As China Roars, Pollution Reaches Deadly Extremes." *New York Times.* 26 Aug. 2007. http://www.nytimes.com/2007/08/26/world/asia/26china.html?pagewanted=print.

efficiency problems and requires twice as much energy to regulate temperature as those in developed countries with similar climates. Indeed, according to the World Bank, 95% of buildings in China don't meet basic Chinese building codes.[23] Overall, China requires seven times the resources Japan does in order to produce the same level of output while even India is three times more productive.

At the end of the day, China's desire for high growth rates, leaves it sitting with a rather false public growth rate. 10 and 11% growth rates are impressive, but considering the fact that pollution externalities eat up an unaccounted for 10% of China's annual GDP[24] real growth rates are probably somewhat lower than the government's estimations. Despite the dire situation, China seems to be in a position where significant growth can continue to take place over the next several years even if reform efforts stagnate, but the fallout of such negligence will eventually catch up to the economic giant. It's hard to tell how well China is really doing in terms of its pollution controls and just how much more the Chinese environment can take. Either way it is clear that there is still a significant problem, and that China needs to intensify its focus on truly sustainable economic development. Otherwise, China's economy may very well suffocate under its own weight.

23. "China's challenge: huge potential for energy savings." *Rockwool*. Sept. 2008. http://www.rockwool.com/energy+efficiency/inspiration+catalogue/efficient+buildings+can+reduce+co2+emissions/china%E2%80%99s+challenge-c3-+huge+potential+for+energy+savings.

24. "Pollution costs equal 10% of China's GDP." *China Daily*. 6 June 2006. http://www.chinadaily.com.cn/china/2006-06/06/content_609350.htm.

Air Quality in the United States Is Improving

United States Environmental Protection Agency

The US Environmental Protection Agency is an agency of the federal government charged with protecting the environment.

Improving air quality and taking action on climate change are priorities for the EPA [US Environmental Protection Agency]. This summary report presents EPA's most recent evaluation of our nation's air quality status and takes a closer look at the relationship between air quality and climate change.

Levels of Six Common Pollutants Continue to Decline

- Cleaner cars, industries, and consumer products have contributed to cleaner air for much of the U.S.

- Since 1990, nationwide air quality has improved significantly for the six common air pollutants. These six pollutants are ground-level ozone, particle pollution ($PM_{2.5}$ and PM_{10}), lead, nitrogen dioxide (NO_2), carbon monoxide (CO), and sulfur dioxide (SO_2). Nationally, air pollution was lower in 2008 than in 1990 for:

  8-hour ozone, by 14 percent

  annual $PM_{2.5}$ (since 2000), by 19 percent

  PM_{10}, by 31 percent

  Lead, by 78 percent

  NO_2, by 35 percent

"Our Nation's Air: Status and Trends Through 2008, Highlights," United States Environmental Protection Agency, February 2010.

8-hour CO, by 68 percent

annual SO_2, by 59 percent

- Despite clean air progress, approximately 127 million people lived in counties that exceeded any national ambient air quality standard (NAAQS) in 2008, . . . Ground-level ozone and particle pollution still present challenges in many areas of the country.

- Nationally, for the period from 2001 to 2008, annual $PM_{2.5}$ concentrations were 17 percent lower in 2008 compared to 2001. 24-hour $PM_{2.5}$ concentrations were 19 percent lower in 2008 compared to 2001.

- Ozone levels did not improve in much of the East until 2002, after which there was a significant decline. 8-hour ozone concentrations were 10 percent lower in 2008 than in 2001. This decline is largely due to reductions in oxides of nitrogen (NO_x) emissions required by EPA's rule to reduce ozone in the East, the NO_x State Implementation Plan (SIP) Call. EPA tracks progress toward meeting these reductions through its NO_x Budget Trading Program.

Levels of Many Toxic Air Pollutants Have Declined

- Toxic air pollutants such as benzene, 1,3-butadiene, styrene, xylenes, and toluene decreased by 5 percent or more per year between 2000 and 2005 at more than half of ambient monitoring sites. Other key contributors to cancer risk, such as carbon tetrachloride, tetrachloroethylene, and 1,4-dichlorobenzene, declined at most sites.

- Total emissions of toxic air pollutants have decreased by approximately 40 percent between 1990 and 2005. Control programs for mobile sources and facilities such as chemical plants, dry cleaners, coke ovens, and incinerators are primarily responsible for these reductions.

EPA expects air quality to continue to improve as recent regulations are fully implemented and states work to meet . . . revised national air quality standards.

Acid Rain and Haze Are Declining

- EPA's NO_x SIP Call and Acid Rain Program have contributed to significant improvements in air quality and environmental health. The required reductions in SO_2 and NO_x have led to significant decreases in atmospheric deposition, which have contributed to improved water quality in lakes and streams. For example, between 1989–1991 and 2006–2008, wet sulfate deposition decreased more than 30 percent and wet nitrate deposition decreased more than 30 percent in parts of the East.

- Between 1998 and 2007, visibility in scenic areas improved throughout the country. Eight areas—Mt. Rainier National Park, WA; Great Gulf Wilderness, NH; Snoqualmie Pass, WA; Olympia, WA; Columbia Gorge, WA; Starkey, OR; Presque Isle, ME, and Bridgton, ME—showed notable improvement on days with the worst visibility.

Climate Change and International Transport: Improving Our Understanding

- In 2007, the U.N. Intergovernmental Panel on Climate Change (IPCC) [an international body created to study and report on climate change] concluded that climate change is happening now, as evident from observations of increases in global average air and ocean temperatures, widespread snow melt, and rising average sea levels.

- Research is continuing to improve our understanding of the effects of air pollution on climate. For example, tropospheric ozone (a greenhouse gas) has a warming effect on climate. Black carbon particle pollution has warming effects, while aerosols containing sulfates and organic carbon tend to have cooling effects. Also, research is continuing to investigate the effects of climate change on future air pollution levels.

- Ongoing studies continue to improve our understanding about air pollution movement between countries and continents.

More Improvements Anticipated

- EPA expects air quality to continue to improve as recent regulations are fully implemented and states work to meet current and recently revised national air quality standards. Key regulations include the Locomotive Engines and Marine Compression-Ignition Engines Rule, the Tier II Vehicle and Gasoline Sulfur Rule, the Heavy-Duty Highway Diesel Rule, the Clean Air Non-Road Diesel Rule, and the Mobile Source Air Toxics Rule.

Drinking Water in the United States Is Safer than It Used to Be

Karen Springen

Karen Springen is a writer for Newsweek, *an American weekly news magazine published in New York City.*

There's no question that drinking water is essential to our survival. But does it matter whether it comes from the sink or the store? Not according to Benjamin Grumbles, head of the U.S. Environmental Protection Agency's [EPA] water programs. "It's an urban myth that bottled water is safer than tap water," he says. "Without a doubt, we have a drinking water system that's the envy of the world."

US Water Standards Have Improved

Until 1962 the federal government had no public drinking water quality standards. But today the EPA requires municipalities to test water daily and validates testing to make sure the nation's 52,000 community water systems meet stringent standards. (Consumers can contact their local water supplier and ask for the annual report card on contaminants.) "Municipalities are required to release a lot of information about what is in the tap water, and they have to test it more frequently than manufacturers of bottled water have to test their water," says Jennifer Hattam, green lifestyles editor for the Sierra Club's magazine.

Bottled water quality standards have been in place for nearly 35 years, and the industry is regulated by the Food and Drug Administration. But even bottled water industry officials don't claim it's better for you than tap water. "We think drink-

Karen Springen, "Is Bottled Water Better Than Tap?" *Newsweek*, December 5, 2007. Used by permission of Newsweek.

ing water, whether it's bottled or tap water, is a good thing. I will not state that bottled water is healthier," says Joe Doss, president of the International Bottled Water Association (IBWA), which represents bottled water makers. Instead the association stresses that there are some "taste differences" and "convenience issues." "It just boils down to what consumers prefer," says Doss.

Bottled or Tap Water?

Judging by the numbers, it seems many prefer their water bottled—at least, some of the time. Last year Americans drank 8.2 billion gallons of bottled water, an increase of 9.5 percent from the year before. But 75 percent of bottled-water consumers report that they drink both water from the tap and bottled water, according to the IBWA. And, especially with a filter, you may not taste a difference. "It's very easy to create the same quality of water from your tap," says Urvashi Rangan, senior scientist and policy analyst for Consumers Union. (If you want more information on filters, check the Natural Resources Defense Council's guide and Consumer Reports' Greenerchoices.org.)

Nearly half of all bottled water comes from the tap, anyway. (The rest use ground water—think "spring" water or "artesian" water.) But bottlers treat the tap water. Bottled water is stripped of chlorine, which is used by municipalities to disinfect tap water and can leave an aftertaste. Many bottled-water producers use ozone or ultraviolet disinfection instead. Bottled water is also stripped of fluoride, which is known to help prevent teeth decay, but many manufacturers add it back to their brands.

While clean water in any form is good for you, tap water is better for the environment. Bottled water is usually packaged in single-use bottles made from fossil fuels, says Janet Larsen, director of research for the Earth Policy Institute in Washington, D.C. And bottled water often travels long distances, which can burn a lot more fuel. This week, the EPA released new data that shows that manufacturing the 29 billion plastic bottles used for water in the United States requires the equivalent of more than 17 million barrels of crude oil.

Tap Water Is a Bargain

When it comes down to it, most people use bottled water sparingly not because it's any healthier or less healthy—but because it's tougher on their pocketbook and on the environment. The EPA's Grumbles drinks bottled water only when he's on airplanes or traveling. "We're a mobile society, so there will always be a need for bottled water," he says. "[But] tap water is a tremendous bargain."

China Is Meeting Its Targets for Reducing Air and Water Pollution

Li Jing

Li Jing is a reporter for China Daily, *an English-language newspaper and related website providing news and business information about China.*

China is beating its targets for reducing major air and water pollution for 2010, Environmental Protection Minister Zhou Shengxian said.

On the back of that success, the country will include two more pollutants into its compulsory emission control program during the 12th Five-Year Plan (2011–15) period.

"China has dramatically boosted its pollution prevention capacity, and is set to meet the emission reductions of sulfur dioxide and chemical oxygen demand between 2005 and 2010," Zhou was quoted as saying on Friday [September 2010] by *People's Daily* at an international forum on environment and development.

Sulfur Dioxide and Air Pollution

Sulfur dioxide is a major indicator of air pollution and carbon oxygen demand is a measurement used to determine the level of water pollution.

By the end of last year, the emission levels of sulfur dioxide had fallen 9.6 percent from 2005 levels, while chemical oxygen demand had fallen 13.1 percent during the same period.

Li Jing, "China's Pollution Reduction Right on Target," *China Daily*, September 18, 2010. Used by permission of China Daily.

That puts China on target to hit its goal of reducing both by 10 percent from 2005 levels by the end of 2010.

In the first half of this year, carbon oxygen demand dropped 2.3 percent year-on-year, but sulfur dioxide levels increased 0.22 percent, according to the Ministry of Environmental Protection.

Nitrogen Oxides and Acid Rain

New goals for nitrogen oxides, which cause acid rain and haze, and ammonia nitrogen, which leads to excessive food sources for bacteria in water bodies, will be included in the pollution control program for next five years, said Zhou.

But detailed reduction targets are yet to be worked out, experts familiar with the matter told *China Daily* on Friday.

Coal-fired power plants are major sources for nitrogen oxides, which contribute 45.5 percent to total emissions, according to Yang Jintian, deputy chief engineer of the Chinese Academy of Environmental Planning.

Official figures from the Ministry of Environmental Protection show that the country's total emissions of nitrogen oxide reached 20 million tons in 2008, the largest in the world.

Nitrogen oxides, when mixed with other air pollutants, can cause chemical reactions that form haze and smog.

"It is impossible to cure haze and acid rain problems in big cities without addressing pollution of nitrogen oxide," said Yang.

New goals for nitrogen oxides . . . and ammonia nitrogen . . . will be included in the pollution control program for next five years.

Ammonia Nitrogen and Algae Growth

The accumulation of ammonia nitrogen in rivers and lakes can lead to excessive nutrition levels in water bodies—which cause the overgrowth of blue and green algae.

"Under certain conditions, ammonia nitrogen can also convert into toxic compounds, which pose threats to drinking water safety," said Fu Qing, an associate professor with Chinese Research Academy of Environmental Sciences.

The pollutant is discharged from chemical plants, agricultural chemicals like fertilizers and pesticides, as well as domestic sewage in urban areas, said Fu.

China discharged 1.23 million tons of ammonia nitrogen in 2009, with 78 percent being from domestic sewage, according to the Ministry of Environmental Protection.

The country will seek to bolster its rapid economic growth with a minimum of environmental degradation and strike a balance between development and conservation, Zhou told the forum held in Beijing.

He said China needs to improve its green economic policies to facilitate the shift to a "highly effective and low-emission" growth mode.

Between 2006 and 2010, more than 10 billion yuan ($1.5 billion) was put into research and development of technologies related to energy conservation and environmental protection, according to Ministry of Science and Technology.

China Is Spending Billions to Ensure Sustainable Water Use

Chaoqing Yu

Chaoqing Yu is an associate professor with the Center for Earth System Science and the Institute for Global Change Studies at Tsinghua University in Beijing, China.

Late last month [January 2011], the Chinese government announced that it will invest four trillion renminbi (US$600 billion) over the next ten years to protect and improve access to water. The policy was [spelled] out in this year's No 1 Document—the central government's first policy document of the year, setting the top priorities—released on 29 January, and comes as a severe and continuing drought in northern China threatens crops of winter wheat.

The Challenges Ahead

The Chinese government is right to highlight sustainable use of water resources as critical for China's food, economic, ecological and even national security. Among the measures it proposes are control of total water consumption, improved irrigation efficiency, restricted groundwater pumping, reduced water pollution and guaranteed funds for water-conservancy projects. Such a national policy could go a long way to help secure and protect China's water. How to put the policy into practice, however, remains challenging.

Since the 1950s, China has constructed 86,000 reservoirs, drilled more than four million wells, and developed 58 million hectares of irrigated land, which generates 70% of the country's total grain production. Efforts to conserve water have lagged far behind. The largest threat to sustainable water

Chaoqing Yu, "China's Water Crisis Needs More than Words," *Nature News*, February 16, 2011. Used by permission of Nature News.

supplies in China is a growing geographical mismatch between agricultural development and water resources. The centre of grain production in China has moved from the humid south to the water-scarce north over the past 30 years, as southern cropland is built on and more land is irrigated further north. As the north has become drier, increased food production there has largely relied on unsustainable overuse of local water resources, especially groundwater. Wasteful irrigation infrastructure, poorly managed water use, as well as fast industrialization and urbanization, have led to serious depletion of groundwater aquifers, loss of natural habitats and water pollution.

> *China needs to build an integrated network to monitor surface and groundwater, and use it to assess and set water policies through an integrated water-resource management system.*

Tackling China's Water Pollution

To tackle water issues in China, one problem that must be addressed is the scattering of authority across different agencies. At present, major rivers are managed by the Ministry of Water Resources, whereas local governments control smaller water courses. Water supply, farmland irrigation, groundwater, water pollution and weather forecasting are separately administrated by, respectively, the Ministry of Housing and Urban-Rural Development, the Ministry of Agriculture, the Ministry of Land and Resources, the Ministry of Environmental Protection, and the State Meteorological Administration.

Data on precipitation, river runoff, groundwater, land use, pollution and water use are not shared between governmental agencies, or made accessible to the public. It will be difficult to implement the holistic policy laid out in the No 1 Document without breaking down these bureaucratic barriers.

As a starting point, China needs to build an integrated network to monitor surface and groundwater, and use it to assess and set water policies through an integrated water-resource management system. And for this to happen, China needs a law that sets out clear policies on data sharing, and penalties for those who do not comply.

Other legislation is needed too. A water law introduced in 1988, and amended in 2002, is too vague to apply in practice, and there remains confusion over water rights of individuals, such as whether to grant them based on land ownership or use.

As political attention to water increases, a new, fair water law, based on transparent decisions, is essential to protect citizens' rights and prevent corruption. Low-income farmers will suffer greatly if water prices rise. To protect them, and so food supplies, China must keep irrigation costs low. Clear measures will also be needed to better match food production with water availability. Without regulation to increase food production in the south, it will be difficult to maintain food security, even if water-use efficiency is improved in the north.

Some of the areas identified in the document need more attention. Despite increasing concern about the effects of climate change on the availability and suitability of water resources, the document does not specifically define adaption to climate impacts. It is also vague on how the departments of water resources and environment protection should cooperate on planned new limits on water pollutants. Ecological water use is mentioned, but the document does not outline the specific measures that will be needed to protect the water supply of ecosystems against conflicting demands of economic activity. The role of ecosystems in water availability must be explicitly accounted for.

How will the money be raised to deliver the government's promises on water? The document demands that local governments reserve 10% of the annual income (currently 70 billion renminbi) from land sales for real-estate development to be used for water projects. However, it is not clear whether this money would be better held by local governments or allocated by Beijing.

The current drought shows how urgent the problem of sustainable water use and supply is for China. Although many of the policies and measures in the No 1 Document are not new and still need more work, the high priority the government has placed on sustainable water use is extremely welcome.

Current CONTROVERSIES

CHAPTER 2

Is Global Warming a Real Environmental Threat?

Chapter Preface

In 1988, the United Nations Environment Programme (UNEP) and the World Meteorological Organization (WMO) established the Intergovernmental Panel on Climate Change (IPCC) and charged it with reviewing all the scientific and technological evidence on global warming. To accomplish this, the IPCC engaged the world's top scientists and climate experts from over sixty countries to assess the science supporting the theory of global warming and advise the world on solutions. To date, the IPCC has published four comprehensive assessments—in 1990, 1996, 2001, and most recently the Fourth Assessment Report (AR4), which was released in 2007. This 2007 report is divided into three sections—"The Physical Science Basis," "Impacts, Adaptation and Vulnerability," and "Mitigation of Climate Change." The next IPCC report, the Fifth Assessment Report (AR5), is expected to be completed in 2013/2014.

The latest IPCC report (AR4) is significant because, for the first time, the organization concluded that it is "unequivocal"[1] that the Earth's climate is warming based on increases in average air and ocean temperatures, widespread melting of snow and ice, and rising global mean sea levels. In addition, the AR4 concluded that it is "very likely"[2] that emissions of greenhouse gases from human activities, such as the burning of fossil fuels, have caused most of the observed climate warming. The report explains that since the beginning of the industrial era, the atmospheric concentrations of carbon dioxide and methane, two of the most potent heat-trapping greenhouse gases, have increased at an unprecedented rate. Today, the IPCC says, the amount of these two gases in the Earth's atmosphere exceeds the natural range over the last 650,000 years.

In recent years, the AR4 concludes, humans have witnessed many of the hallmarks of climate change, including rising temperatures, increasingly severe weather, more melting and thawing of glaciers and snow covers, and rising sea levels. For example, the report explains that eleven out of the last twelve years have been the hottest on record since measurements began in 1850, with hot days and heat waves becoming more and more frequent. In addition, storms, precipitation, and drought have become more pronounced. Tropical cyclones and hurricanes have become more intense in the North Atlantic Ocean; heavy rainstorms are more frequent in some areas of North and South America, Europe, and Asia; and droughts have made other areas in Africa, the Mediterranean region, and Asia much dryer and less fertile.

Other indications that climate change is happening, the IPCC explains, can be found in rising sea levels and the loss of glaciers, sea ice, and snow. According to the AR4, the Northern Hemisphere has lost 7 percent of its maximum seasonally frozen ground since 1900. Mountain glaciers and snow cover have also declined on a global scale, and summer sea ice has shrunk more than 20 percent since 1978. In addition, the IPCC says that sea levels have risen. Partly, this is caused by the melting glaciers and ice sheets, but the world's oceans have also been absorbing much of the heat caused by climate change, resulting in an expansion of ocean water.

According to the AR4, the future progression of climate change depends on the levels of greenhouse gas emissions. The report projected six possible scenarios with varying levels of emissions. The best case scenario—which assumes a midcentury global population peak and a rapid shift toward clean energy technologies—estimates a 3.2 degree Fahrenheit rise in average global temperatures by 2090. The worst case scenario—which similarly assumes a midcentury population peak but continued intensive fossil fuel energy production and consumption—projects a 7.2 degree Fahrenheit rise in average global temperatures by 2090. The IPCC warns, however, that these are best estimates, and that it is possible that temperatures could increase even more if no action is taken to reduce greenhouse gas emissions.

In fact, even if humans act immediately to dramatically reduce global warming emissions, the Earth will continue to warm because the effects of past emissions will last for decades. The IPCC says our future, therefore, will most certainly feature even hotter temperatures; more frequent and increasingly severe weather patterns such as hurricanes, heavy rain and snowstorms, heat waves, and droughts; faster melting of glaciers and sea ice; and ocean changes such as acidification, slower ocean currents, and significant seawater warming.

The IPCC findings have been embraced by most of the world's scientists, but in recent years the climate change theory and projections have been questioned in the media by a number of global warming skeptics. These skeptics generally dispute the notion that climate change is caused by human activities and are opposed to the enactment of public policies that could limit greenhouse gas emissions. The doubts raised by climate change deniers received a boost in 2009 when a series of scientists' e-mails surfaced that skeptics said revealed manipulation of climate data. Most scientific experts concluded that the e-mails did not show serious scientific misconduct or change the basic IPCC findings about climate change, but the controversy continues nevertheless. The authors in this chapter address this critical question of whether global warming is a real environmental threat.

Notes

1. Intergovernmental Panel on Climate Change, "Climate Change 2007: Synthesis Report, Summary for Policymakers," November 2007, p. 2. www.ipcc.ch/pdf/assessment -report/ar4/syr/ar4_syr_spm.pdf.

2. Intergovernmental Panel on Climate Change, "Climate Change 2007: Synthesis Report, Summary for Policymakers," November 2007, p. 5. www.ipcc.ch/pdf/assessment -report/ar4/syr/ar4_syr_spm.pdf.

Science Provides a Compelling Case that Global Warming Is Real

America's Climate Choices: Panel on Advancing the Science of Climate Change

America's Climate Choices is a group of activities arranged by the National Research Council, an organization that advises the federal government about science and technology, to study issues associated with global climate change. The Panel on Advancing the Science of Climate Change is a part of this effort and was charged with providing a concise overview of climate change science and the scientific advances needed to respond to future climate challenges.

Science has made enormous inroads in understanding climate change and its causes, and is beginning to help develop a strong understanding of current and potential imparts that will affect people today and in coming decades. This understanding is crucial because it allows decision makers to place climate change in the context of other large challenges facing the nation and the world. There are still some uncertainties, and there always will be in understanding a complex system like Earth's climate. Nevertheless, there is a strong, credible body of evidence, based on multiple lines of research, documenting that climate is changing and that these changes are in large part caused by human activities. While much remains to be learned, the core phenomenon, scientific questions, and hypotheses have been examined thoroughly and have stood firm in the face of serious scientific debate and careful evaluation of alternative explanations.

As a result of the growing recognition that climate change is under way and poses serious risks for both human societies

Board on Atmospheric Sciences and Climate, "Summary," Advancing the Science of Climate Change, 2010. Used by permission.

and natural systems, the question that decision makers are asking has expanded from "What is happening?" to "What is happening and what can we do about it?". Scientific research can help answer both of these important questions. In addition to the extensive body of research on the causes and consequences of climate change, there is a growing body of knowledge about technologies and policies that can be used to limit the magnitude of future climate change, a smaller but expanding understanding of the steps that can be taken to adapt to climate change, and a growing recognition that climate change will need to be considered in actions and decisions across a wide range of sectors and interests. . . .

Most of the warming over the last several decades can be attributed to human activities that release carbon dioxide (CO_2) and other heat-trapping greenhouse gases (GHGs) into the atmosphere.

[A] report [by the National Research Council, an organization that advises Congress on science and technology], *Advancing the Science of Climate Change*, reviews the current scientific evidence regarding climate change and examines the status of the nation's scientific research efforts. It also describes the critical role that climate change science, broadly defined, can play in developing knowledge and tools to assist decision makers as they act to respond to climate change. The report explores seven crosscutting research themes that should be included in the nation's climate change research enterprise and recommends a number of actions to advance the science of climate change—a science that includes and increasingly integrates across the physical, biological, social, health, and engineering sciences. Overall, the report concludes that:

1. Climate change is occurring, is caused largely by human activities, and poses significant risks for a broad range of human and natural systems; and

2. The nation needs a comprehensive and integrated climate change science enterprise, one that not only contributes to our fundamental understanding of climate change but also informs and expands America's climate choices.

What We Know About Climate Change

Conclusion 1: Climate change is occurring, is caused largely by human activities, and poses significant risks for—and in many cases is already affecting—a broad range of human and natural systems.

This conclusion is based on a substantial array of scientific evidence, including recent work, and is consistent with the conclusions of recent assessments by the U.S. Global Change Research Program, the Intergovernmental Panel on Climate Change's Fourth Assessment Report, and other assessments of the state of scientific knowledge on climate change. Both our assessment . . . and these previous assessments place high or very high confidence in the following findings:

- Earth is warming. Detailed observations of surface temperature assembled and analyzed by several different research groups show that the planet's average surface temperature was 1.4°F (0.8°C) warmer during the first decade of the 21st century than during the first decade of the 20th century, with the most pronounced warming over the past three decades. These data are corroborated by a variety of independent observations that indicate warming in other parts of the Earth system, including the cryosphere (snow- and ice-covered regions), the lower atmosphere, and the oceans.

- Most of the warming over the last several decades can be attributed to human activities that release carbon dioxide (CO_2) and other heat-trapping greenhouse gases (GHGs) into the atmosphere. The burning of fossil fuels—coal, oil, and natural gas—for energy is the single largest human driver of climate change, but agriculture, forest clearing, and certain industrial activities also make significant contributions.

- Natural climate variability leads to year-to-year and decade-to-decade fluctuations in temperature and other climate variables, as well as substantial regional differences, but cannot explain or offset the long-term warming trend.

- Global warming is closely associated with a broad spectrum of other changes, such as increases in the frequency of intense rainfall, decreases in Northern Hemisphere snow cover and Arctice sea ice, warmer and more frequent hot days and nights, rising sea levels, and widespread ocean acidification.

- Human-induced climate change and its impacts will continue for many decades, and in some cases for many centuries. Individually and collectively, these changes pose risks for a wide range of human and environmental systems, including freshwater resources, the coastal environment, ecosystems, agriculture, fisheries, human health, and national security, among others.

- The ultimate magnitude of climate change and the severity of its impacts depend strongly on the actions that human societies take to respond to these risks.

Projections of future climate change depend strongly on how human societies decide to produce and use energy and other resources in the decades ahead.

Despite an international agreement to stabilize GHG concentrations "at levels that would avoid dangerous anthropogenic interference with the climate system", global emissions of

CO_2 and several other GHGs continue to increase. Projections of future climate change, which are based on computer models of how the climate system would respond to different scenarios of future human activities, anticipate an additional warming of 2.0°F to 11.5°F (1.1°C to 6.4°C) over the 21st century. A separate National Research Council (NRC) report, *Climate Stabilization Targets: Emissions, Concentrations, and Impacts over Decades to Millennia*, provides an analysis of expected impacts at different magnitudes of future warming.

In general, it is reasonable to expect that the magnitude of future climate change and the severity of its impacts will be larger if actions are not taken to reduce GHG emissions and adapt to its impacts. However, as with all projections of the future, there will always be some uncertainty regarding the details of future climate change. Several factors contribute to this uncertainty:

- Projections of future climate change depend strongly on how human societies decide to produce and use energy and other resources in the decades ahead.

- Human-caused changes in climate overlap with natural climate variability, especially at regional scales.

- Certain Earth system processes—including the carbon cycle, ice sheet dynamics, and cloud and aerosol processes—are not yet completely understood or fully represented in climate models but could potentially have a strong influence on future climate changes.

- Climate change impacts typically play out at local to regional scales, but processes at these scales are not as well represented by models as continental- to global-scale changes.

- The impacts of climate change depend on how climate change interacts with other global and regional environmental changes, including changes in land use, management of natural resources, and emissions of other pollutants.

- The impacts of climate change also depend critically on the vulnerability and adaptive capacity of human and natural systems, which can vary widely in space and time and generally are not as well understood as changes in the physical climate system.

Climate change also poses challenges that set it apart from other risks with which people normally deal. For example, many climate change processes have considerable inertia and long time lags, so it is mainly future generations that will have to deal with the consequences (both positive and negative) of decisions made today. Also, rather than smooth and gradual climate shifts, there is the potential that the Earth system could cross tipping points or thresholds that result in abrupt changes. Some of the greatest risks posed by climate change are associated with these abrupt changes and other climate "surprises" (unexpected changes or impacts), yet the likelihood of such events is not well known. Moreover, there has been comparatively little research on the impacts that might be associated with "extreme" climate change—for example, the impacts that could be expected if global temperatures rise by 10°F (6°C) or more over the next century. Thus, while it seems clear that the Earth's future climate will be unlike the climate that ecosystems and human societies have become accustomed to during the last 10,000 years, the exact magnitude of future climate change and the nature of its impacts will always remain somewhat uncertain.

Decision makers of all types, including businesses, governments, and individual citizens, are beginning to take actions to reduce the risks posed by climate change—including actions to limit its magnitude and actions to adapt to its impacts. Effective management of climate risks will require decision makers to take actions that are flexible and robust, to learn from new knowledge and experience, and to adjust future actions accordingly. The long time lags associated with climate change and the presence of differential vulnerabilities and capacities to respond to climate change likewise represent formidable management challenges. These challenges also have significant implications for the nation's climate science enterprise.

A New Era of Climate Change Research

Conclusion 2: The nation needs a comprehensive and integrative climate change science enterprise, one that not only contributes to our fundamental understanding of climate change but also informs and expands America's climate choices.

Research efforts over the past several decades have provided a wealth of information to decision makers about the known and potential risks posed by climate change. Experts from a diverse range of disciplines have also identified and developed a variety of actions that could be taken to limit the magnitude of future climate change or adapt to its impacts. However, much remains to be learned. Continued investments in scientific research can be expected to improve our understanding of the causes and consequences of climate change. In addition, the nation's research enterprise could potentially play a much larger role in addressing questions of interest to decision makers as they develop, evaluate, and execute plans to respond to climate change. Because decisions always involve value judgments, science cannot prescribe the decisions that should be made. However, scientific research can play a key role by informing decisions and by expanding and improving the portfolio of available options.

There Is No Reason to Doubt Basic Global Warming

Mark Lynas

Mark Lynas is an environmental activist and a climate change specialist. His books on the subject include High Tide: The Truth About Our Climate Crisis *and* Six Degrees: Our Future on a Hotter Planet.

The arguments of climate sceptics have largely been moulded by a far more sinister force—the US-based conservative think tanks.

Global Emissions Are Rising

I am finding it increasingly difficult to maintain my optimism that we can stabilise global temperature increases below the "danger level" of 2°C [Celsius]. First, there is no sign that emissions are being reduced; rather, the opposite is happening. Second, it is becoming clear that the danger level for temperature increase is a good deal lower than 2°C.

The Arctic Sea ice cover is already approaching a new low. The new topic of speculation is not whether the Arctic ice will disappear completely in the summer months by 2080, but whether this will happen by 2018. An ice-free North Pole will have a significant effect on the planet's energy balance, given the important role this huge white "mirror" plays in reflecting incoming solar radiation. Once it is gone, the warming process can only speed up further. Already, a new study suggests that an ice-free Arctic Ocean will dramatically increase warming in surrounding land areas, accelerating the degradation of permafrost and resulting in huge releases of carbon and methane—driving yet more warming. Setting a danger level of 2°C,

Mark Lynas, "The Global Warming Deniers," *New Statesman*, July 3, 2008. Used by permission.

as the UK [United Kingdom] and EU [European Union] have done, now looks dangerously optimistic.

The Intergovernmental Panel on Climate Change (IPCC) reported last year that emissions cuts within a decade could still keep temperature hikes below 2°C. But global emissions are rising year on year, not falling. Many climate models are underpinned by an assumption of 1.5 per cent increases annually in carbon releases. Instead, they have been running at more than 2 per cent.

A MORI poll reported by the Observer *last month found six out of ten people think, wrongly, that "many scientific experts" disagree on whether human beings are causing climate change.*

In the words of the Tyndall Centre scientist Kevin Anderson: "Since 2000 the world has gone ballistic in terms of carbon emissions." Anderson has recently revised his projections for climate change and now thinks that the "best we can expect" is stabilising atmospheric concentrations at 650 parts per million CO_2 [carbon dioxide] equivalent, equating to warming of about 4°C. He suggests we "mitigate for 2°, but adapt for 4°".

Adapting to 4°C of warming would be quite a challenge. With this level of temperature change, we can expect a huge increase in drought-prone zones, a mass extinction of half or more of the life on earth, hundreds of millions of refugees from areas deprived of fresh water or inundated by rising seas, and widespread starvation due to food and water shortages.

The Denial Lobby

The Stockholm Network's *Carbon Scenarios* report (which I helped draft) reaches a similar conclusion, projecting a warming of nearly 5°C if global policy on climate continues to fail.

Against this terrifying backdrop, the denial lobby flourishes, its success almost calling into question the capacity of mankind for reasoned thought.

Nigel Lawson's dreadful book, laughably entitled *An Appeal to Reason*, has been riding high in the sales charts and is only one of several denialist tomes on global warming. The last time I looked, four out of five of Amazon's top sellers on climate were penned by deniers. And these are not just views from the fringe. A MORI poll reported by the *Observer* last month [June 2008] found six out of ten people think, wrongly, that "many scientific experts" disagree on whether human beings are causing climate change. Four out of ten people asked believed that the impact had been exaggerated.

Many climate-change sceptics like to think they are proudly independent people, refusing to be cowed by UN [United Nations]-sponsored orthodoxy from the IPCC. In fact, the arguments of climate sceptics have largely been moulded by a far more sinister force—the US-based conservative think tanks. A recent academic survey of environmentally sceptical books found that 92 per cent were linked with these think tanks, which include the Heritage Foundation, the Cato Institute and the Competitive Enterprise Institute. Since the early 1990s, these and other industry-funded front groups have been leading an anti-environmental backlash, changing the tenor of the political debate on environmental issues and bombarding the media and the public with disinformation.

Politics and Public Perception

The authors of the study, published in the June edition of a journal called *Environmental Politics*, argue that, far from being a true grass-roots movement, "environmental scepticism is an elite-driven reaction to global environmentalism, organised by core actors within the conservative movement". The "self-portrayal of sceptics as marginalised 'Davids' battling the powerful 'Goliath' of environmentalists and environmental scientists is a charade", given that the "sceptics are supported by politically powerful conservative think tanks funded by wealthy foundations and corporations".

Next time someone insists global warming isn't happening, ask yourself where their views come from—and whose interests they serve.

Record US Temperatures in 2010 Are Consistent with Global Warming Predictions

Pete Spotts

Pete Spotts is a science reporter for the Christian Science Monitor, *an international news organization.*

Last year [2010] tied 2005 as the warmest year on record, federal climatologists said Wednesday [January 12, 2011], adding that an analysis of the year's data strengthened the notion that greenhouse gases from burning fossil fuels are continuing to warm Earth's climate.

According to a preliminary analysis of year-end data released Wednesday, the global average temperature in 2010 topped the 20th century average by 1.12 degrees Fahrenheit [F].

This caps a decade marked by nine of the 10 warmest years on record and represents the 34th consecutive year in which global average temperatures topped the 20th-century average, according to data compiled by the National Oceanic and Atmospheric Administration's [NOAA] Climatic Data Center in Asheville, N.C.

In addition, the year was the wettest on record globally, although rain and snowfall varied widely from place to place.

A moderate-to-strong El Nino pattern in the eastern Pacific and a similarly energetic La Nina that followed played key roles in 2010 in setting up conditions that contributed both to temperature and precipitation patterns during the year.

Pete Spotts, "Global Warming Waning? Hardly. 2010 Was Tied as Warmest Year on Record," *Christian Science Monitor*, January 12, 2011. Used by permission.

The two patterns alternate over periods of two to seven years in the tropical Pacific. El Nino brings an expanse of warm water from the western Pacific to a region of the ocean off northern South America, while La Nina replaces the warm water with unusually cold water. These swings trigger changes in atmospheric circulation patterns that, while most prominent in the tropics, also affect circulation patterns at higher latitudes as well.

There has been some notion people have put forth that the climate stopped warming in about 2005. This years' results show that notion lacks credibility.

But while these natural swings in Earth's climate played important roles in shaping seasonal weather patterns, as well as the year's global-temperature ranking, NOAA officials say, so has global warming—particularly over the past 30 to 40 years.

Climate Has Not Stopped Warming

"There has been some notion people have put forth that the climate stopped warming in about 2005. This years' results show that notion lacks credibility," said David Easterling, who heads the Climatic Data Center's scientific services division. Instead, he says, the year-end analysis "reinforces the notion that we're seeing an influence on the climate by greenhouse gases."

That might seem counterintuitive to residents of the US South, for instance, who are still thawing out from heavy snows. But researchers caution against confusing a seasonal storm with climate, which is a decade- to centuries-long average of temperature, precipitation, and other atmospheric conditions.

"Climate change is a global phenomenon and a long-term phenomenon," Dr. Easterling explains. Unusually cold temperatures, such as those the Eastern US has experienced over the past two winters, merely reflect natural variations that are superimposed on the much-longer-term warming trend. Global climate—changing or relatively stable—encompasses much more in time and space than a winter Nor'easter burying New England under a foot or more of snow.

Data for 2010 also revealed a warm and wet year on average for the continental United States, according to the data center's analysis.

Heavy snow in the East last February and record warmth in the summer along the southeast and into New England "were two fairly remarkable events," said Derek Arndt, who heads the center's climate monitoring branch.

Extra Precipitation Had Benefits

Rain and snowfall over the US in 2010 topped the long-term precipitation average by 1.02 inches, while 2010 marked the 14th consecutive year when the average annual temperature topped the long-term average.

That extra precipitation provided some tangible benefits, reducing the extent of areas experiencing drought to roughly 8 percent of the country by July. At the same time the moisture contributed to fewer wildfires. By fall, however, drought conditions began to expand into the South.

So far, the average annual temperature in the US has been rising about 0.12 degrees F per decade since 1895, while precipitation has been rising by around 0.18 inches a decade.

Record Cold and Snowstorms of 2010 Do Not Disprove Global Warming

Wendy Koch

Wendy Koch is a reporter for USA Today, a widely circulated national American daily newspaper.

While the [2010] Winter Olympics are about to begin in a Vancouver [Canada] with little snow, the [US] East Coast's blizzard—also known as snowmageddon, snowpocalypse, snowoverit and snOMG—is firing up debate about global warming.

Climate Skeptics vs. Climate Scientists

Nowhere is this more intense than in the nation's capital, President [Barack] Obama's new hometown, which has had an unprecedented three feet of snow in the last week [February 6–11, 2010]. The federal government shut down Thursday [February 11, 2010] for the fourth consecutive day.

"It's going to keep snowing in DC until Al Gore cries 'uncle,'" Sen. Jim DeMint, R-S.C., wrote Wednesday on Twitter.

The family of Sen. James Inhofe, R-Okla., another global warming skeptic, built a six-foot-tall igloo on Capitol Hill and put a cardboard sign on top that read "Al Gore's New Home." Inhofe said the snow reinforced doubts about climate change, reports the *New York Times*.

Also poking fun is [commentator] Matt Drudge who noted on his online Drudge Report that the snowstorm prompted the cancellation this week of a Senate hearing on global warming.

Wendy Koch, "Is Global Warming Real? Do Snowstorms Offer Eco-Lessons?" *USA Today*, February 11, 2011. Used by permission.

Climate scientists have gone on the defensive, arguing that recent extreme weather—including downpours in southern California—do not prove global warming isn't real.

"It's part of natural variability," Gerald Meehl, a senior scientist at the National Center for Atmospheric Research in Boulder, Colo., recently told the Associated Press. With global warming in some areas, he said, "we'll still have record cold temperatures. We'll just have fewer of them."

In his Weather Underground blog, meteorologist Jeff Masters says global temperators are rising over time and they could actually mean "more intense Nor'easters for the U.S. Mid-Atlantic and Northeast, thanks to the higher levels of moisture present in the air."

A Needed Timeout

So what, if any, eco-lessons do these snowstorms offer? How about the viability of telecommuting, the benefits of smart growth and the value of home?

Despite the federal government's closure, telecommuting made it possible for many federal employees to work from home, *The Washington Post* reports.

Also working from home were many staffers, myself included, of *USA TODAY*, which has its headquarters in the Washington suburb of McLean, Va.

Global [warming] . . . could actually mean "more intense Nor'easters for the U.S. Mid-Atlantic and Northeast, thanks to the higher levels of moisture present in the air."

Not surprisingly, people who live in more urban areas seemed to have an easier time digging out and getting around, suggesting another benefit of smart growth.

Washington Post columnist Sally Quinn, who lives in Washington's Georgetown neighborhood, writes about her long, quiet walk around the white-covered nation's capital:

I have never seen Washington like this before. First of all, it is beautiful. Secondly, it is peaceful—a pervading sense of calm. It's as if I, for one, have been liberated from my daily struggles. I have simply given in to what is happening around me and accepted it. This is unusual for me, to say the least. . . .

For those who haven't been hurt by the blizzard, this has been more like a time to reflect, to meditate and to embrace the silence. . . .

The toxicity, rancor and division we have seen building up recently here were gone, dissipated, purified. The government was shut down, the Congress, too. The religious might say God was calling for a timeout. We needed this.

There Are Many Reasons to Doubt Global Warming Science

Ben Lieberman

Ben Lieberman is a commentator, writer, and senior policy analyst for energy and the environment at the Heritage Foundation, a conservative think tank in Washington, DC.

Global-warming skeptics were hit with numerous setbacks over the past few years—from a major 2007 U.N. [United Nations] report that seemingly confirmed the warming crisis, to [former Vice President] Al Gore's popularization of this gloomy message through his book and Oscar-winning documentary, "An Inconvenient Truth."

And let's not forget the shifting political winds that elected a greener Congress and brought in an administration that made climate change a priority.

But now those skeptics are facing a new challenge: overconfidence.

That's because everything of late has been breaking their way.

OK, overconfidence may be an exaggeration, but the wheels are really coming off the global-warming cart.

Climategate and Other Scandals

"Climategate"—the recent leak of e-mails showing gross misconduct among scientists with key roles in the U.N. report—raises serious questions about how much of the global-warming science we can trust. The scientists were, after all, manipulating the temperature data to show more warming and subverting requests by independent researchers to see the underlying data.

Ben Lieberman, "The Late Great Global Warming Scare," *Washington Times*, February 12, 2010. Used by permission of the author.

Other scary claims in the U.N. report, such as the assertion that Himalayan glaciers are on pace to melt completely by 2035, also turned out to be false and have been retracted recently.

The number who believe global warming is real is dropping, and the number who consider it a crisis has plummeted.

Climategate and other scandals only add to the reasons for doubt. At the same time, Mr. Gore's many terrifying predictions are not withstanding the test of time. His book and movie really played up the supposed link between global warming and Hurricane Katrina. Unfortunately for the scaremongers (and fortunately for those who live on the coast) we haven't seen anything even close to Katrina since. The 2006 through 2008 hurricane seasons were at or below average, and the 2009 season went down as the weakest in more than a decade. So much for a global-warming-induced hurricane trend—and many other such scares.

Another thing missing from the global-warming crisis? Global warming. Temperatures have been flat for more than a decade, and 2009 adds one more year to that trend.

An End to the Global Warming Scare

Polling shows that the American people increasingly see Mr. Gore (and others) as the boy who cried wolf, and they are drawing their own common-sense conclusions. The number who believe global warming is real is dropping, and the number who consider it a crisis has plummeted.

Also declining is the number of those willing to accept substantially higher gasoline prices and electric bills—the intended result of domestic global-warming bills or international treaties that raise the price of fossil fuels so we are forced to use less.

Even studies conducted by the [Barack] Obama administration find reduced economic activity, higher energy prices and lost jobs from such measures. In other words, global-warming policy promises plenty of economic pain for little if any environmental gain—a hard sell at any time, but especially now, given the lingering recession.

For all their stated concern for the issue, President Obama and Congress have an uphill climb to turn this into law. Consider one recent poll, conducted by the Pew Research Center for the People and the Press, asking the American people to rank 20 issues in terms of importance.

Global warming came in 20th—dead last—while the economy came in at No. 1. It won't be easy to enact a law or yoke the U.S. to a global treaty that addresses America's No. 20 priority at the expense of No. 1—and do so in an election year.

There is still plenty to worry skeptics. One example: the Environmental Protection Agency's attempt to impose global-warming policy through costly regulations. Also, there's no room for complacency so long as the forces in favor of global-warming measures remain powerful and persistent. But the facts—and the politics on this issue—are moving away from alarm. We may look back on 2010 as the year when the great global-warming scare really started to fade into history.

Global Warming Theory Is Based on False Science

David Evans

David Evans, who has a PhD in electrical engineering, worked from 1999 to 2006 for the Australian Greenhouse Office, an agency of the Australian government, designing a carbon accounting system.

The debate about global warming has reached ridiculous proportions and is full of micro-thin half-truths and misunderstandings. I am a scientist who was on the carbon gravy train, understands the evidence, was once an alarmist, but am now a skeptic. Watching this issue unfold has been amusing but, lately, worrying. This issue is tearing society apart, making fools out of our politicians.

No Evidence for Global Warming Theory

Let's set a few things straight.

The whole idea that carbon dioxide is the main cause of the recent global warming is based on a guess that was proved false by empirical evidence during the 1990s. But the gravy train was too big, with too many jobs, industries, trading profits, political careers, and the possibility of world government and total control riding on the outcome. So rather than admit they were wrong, the governments, and their tame climate scientists, now outrageously maintain the fiction that carbon dioxide is a dangerous pollutant.

Let's be perfectly clear. Carbon dioxide is a greenhouse gas, and other things being equal, the more carbon dioxide in the air, the warmer the planet. Every bit of carbon dioxide that we emit warms the planet. But the issue is not whether carbon dioxide warms the planet, but how much.

David Evans, "Carbon Warming Too Minor to Be Worth Worrying About," *Financial Post*, April 7, 2011. Used by permission of the author.

Most scientists, on both sides, also agree on how much a given increase in the level of carbon dioxide raises the planet's temperature, if just the extra carbon dioxide is considered. These calculations come from laboratory experiments; the basic physics have been well known for a century.

The disagreement comes about what happens next.

The planet reacts to that extra carbon dioxide, which changes everything. Most critically, the extra warmth causes more water to evaporate from the oceans. But does the water hang around and increase the height of moist air in the atmosphere, or does it simply create more clouds and rain? Back in 1980, when the carbon dioxide theory started, no one knew. The alarmists guessed that it would increase the height of moist air around the planet, which would warm the planet even further, because the moist air is also a greenhouse gas.

The alarmist case [for global warming] is based on [a guess about elevated] moisture in the atmosphere, and there is simply no evidence for the amplification that is at the core of their alarmism.

This is the core idea of every official climate model: For each bit of warming due to carbon dioxide, they claim it ends up causing three bits of warming due to the extra moist air. The climate models amplify the carbon dioxide warming by a factor of three—so two-thirds of their projected warming is due to extra moist air (and other factors); only one-third is due to extra carbon dioxide.

That's the core of the issue. All the disagreements and misunderstandings spring from this. The alarmist case is based on this guess about moisture in the atmosphere, and there is simply no evidence for the amplification that is at the core of their alarmism.

Weather balloons had been measuring the atmosphere since the 1960s, many thousands of them every year. The climate models all predict that as the planet warms, a hot spot of moist air will develop over the tropics about 10 kilometres up, as the layer of moist air expands upwards into the cool dry air above. During the warming of the late 1970s, '80s and '90s, the weather balloons found no hot spot. None at all. Not even a small one. This evidence proves that the climate models are fundamentally flawed, that they greatly overestimate the temperature increases due to carbon dioxide.

This evidence first became clear around the mid-1990s.

At this point, official "climate science" stopped being a science. In science, empirical evidence always trumps theory, no matter how much you are in love with the theory. If theory and evidence disagree, real scientists scrap the theory. But official climate science ignored the crucial weather balloon evidence, and other subsequent evidence that backs it up, and instead clung to their carbon dioxide theory—that just happens to keep them in well-paying jobs with lavish research grants, and gives great political power to their government masters.

Climate models are fundamentally flawed, . . . [because] they greatly overestimate the temperature increases due to carbon dioxide.

What the Climate Science Really Shows

There are now several independent pieces of evidence showing that the earth responds to the warming due to extra carbon dioxide by dampening the warming. Every long-lived natural system behaves this way, counteracting any disturbance. Otherwise the system would be unstable. The climate system is no exception, and now we can prove it.

But the alarmists say the exact opposite, that the climate system amplifies any warming due to extra carbon dioxide, and is potentially unstable. It is no surprise that their predictions of planetary temperature made in 1988 to the U.S. Congress, and again in 1990, 1995, and 2001, have all proved much higher than reality.

They keep lowering the temperature increases they expect, from 0.30C per decade in 1990, to 0.20C per decade in 2001, and now 0.15C per decade—yet they have the gall to tell us "it's worse than expected." These people are not scientists. They overestimate the temperature increases due to carbon dioxide, selectively deny evidence, and now they conceal the truth.

One way they conceal is in the way they measure temperature.

The official thermometers are often located in the warm exhaust of air conditioning outlets, over hot tarmac at airports where they get blasts of hot air from jet engines, at waste-water plants where they get warmth from decomposing sewage, or in hot cities choked with cars and buildings. Global warming is measured in 10ths of a degree, so any extra heating nudge is important. In the United States, nearly 90% of official thermometers surveyed by volunteers violate official siting requirements that they not be too close to an artificial heating source.

Global temperature is also measured by satellites, which measure nearly the whole planet 24/7 without bias. The satellites say the hottest recent year was 1998, and that since 2001 the global temperature has levelled off. Why does official science track only the surface thermometer results and not mention the satellite results?

The Earth has been in a warming trend since the depth of the Little Ice Age around 1680. Human emissions of carbon dioxide were negligible before 1850 and have nearly all come after the Second World War, so human carbon dioxide cannot possibly have caused the trend. Within the trend, the Pacific Decadal Oscillation causes alternating global warming and cooling for 25 to 30 years at a go in each direction. We have just finished a warming phase, so expect mild global cooling for the next two decades.

We are now at an extraordinary juncture. Official climate science, which is funded and directed entirely by government, promotes a theory that is based on a guess about moist air that is now a known falsehood. Governments gleefully accept their advice, because the only ways to curb emissions are to impose taxes and extend government control over all energy use. And to curb emissions on a world scale might even lead to world government—how exciting for the political class!

Even if we stopped emitting all carbon dioxide tomorrow, completely shut up shop and went back to the Stone Age, according to the official government climate models it would be cooler in 2050 by about 0.015 degrees. But their models exaggerate 10-fold—in fact our sacrifices would make the planet in 2050 a mere 0.0015 degrees cooler!

Finally, to those who still believe the planet is in danger from our carbon dioxide emissions: Sorry, but you've been had. Yes, carbon dioxide is a cause of global warming, but it's so minor it's not worth doing much about.

The Winter of 2011 Shows the World Is Cooling, Not Warming

Alan Caruba

Alan Caruba is a writer and blogger who frequently criticizes global warming science.

For New Yorkers and those in my part of New Jersey across the river, snow has fallen eight times since December 14 [2010], an average of once every five days, 56.1 inches in Central Park as of Jan 27th [2011], and people are, shall we say, taking notice?

Along with the snow comes power outages, disrupted bus schedules, air travel delays, commuting by car becomes an auto body repair business bonanza, schools shut their doors, and some people die from weather-related accidents or just from trying to shovel the snow from the driveway.

Having battled the "global warming" hoax since it was first perpetrated in the late 1980s, I have had the good fortune to make friends with many of the world's top meteorologists and climatologists who joined in the long effort to educate people to the fact that there never was a rapid rise in the planet's overall temperatures.

Even so, some mainstream media news outlets have continued to file stories incredulously blaming the winter snow storms on "global warming." The hoax for too many media folk has long since become a religion in which blind faith replaces the objective fact obvious to everyone. It is cold. There is snow. Lots of it.

Alan Caruba, "The Long Winter of 2010–2011," *Back to Basics*, January 28, 2011. Used by permission of the author.

Indeed, the Earth has been in a cooling cycle since around 1998 as verified by meteorological satellite and other data. Piers Corbyn, an astrophysicist and leading forecaster, said "We're now headed for a Maunder minimum of very low solar activity. The globe will be much cooler until about 2035, so there will be a lot more of these cold winters in Europe and the USA."

Considering how the climatologists and meteorologists of the United Nations Intergovernmental Panel on Climate Change have been telling everyone for decades of a coming warming, why should we believe Corbyn and others predicting decades of cold weather? Corbyn studies solar cycles and they determine how warm or cold the Earth is.

It's the Sun, Stupid

Corbyn's astonishing record of accuracy has put his native England's meteorological service to shame for deliberately misleading the British to believe the "global warming" hoax. Not given to vague talk, Corbyn recently said, "The claim that 2010 is the second warmest year on record is delusional, irrelevant and disingenuous. Warmist (warm is cold) explanations for extreme events are as useless as saying 'Wet days cause rain.'"

It is useful to keep in mind that U.S. agencies such as NASA [National Aeronautics and Space Administration] and NOAA [National Oceanic and Atmospheric Administration] have been issuing similar politically correct and meteorologically incorrect "global warming" claims for years.

Consider weather events just since the beginning of the year.

For the first time since 1945, the maximum daytime temperature in North Korea has remained below zero for nearly a month. In neighboring China, the snowfall in northwest China was accompanied by extreme cold and a snowfall that flattened or damaged 100,000 homes. All around the world there have been similar reports, including sunny Italy that set new cold records, -48.3 degrees on January 19.

In the United States, Minnesota shattered its cold records on January 21 reaching an astonishing -46 degrees. In Florida, eight new record lows were set by January 17 and there was snow in every State of the lower 48. And spring will not debut until March 21!

It's not like this is a new weather phenomenon. As any meteorologist will tell you, the Earth has gone through numerous warming and cooling cycles. In its 4.5 billion years, scientists estimate there have been at least seventeen full-blown Great Ice Ages. In near past history, the last Little Ice Age is well documented, having begun around 1300 and not ended until 1850. Whatever warming occurred since then, however, has amounted to just over one degree, but that was enough!

As in previous cooling cycles, it was low solar activity that determined the temperature [in recent years], not carbon dioxide or other so-called greenhouse gases.

Reaching its peak in the 17th century, in England the Thames River froze over. The Little Ice Age is credited with bringing down the French monarchy and ruining Napoleon's subsequent Russia campaign. In America, the tiny army of George Washington weathered a harsh winter at Valley Forge.

As in previous cooling cycles, it was low solar activity that determined the temperature, not carbon dioxide or other so-called greenhouse gases.

People's lives depend on our government's ability to measure and forecast the weather. A government that continues to tell people that "global warming" is real and then throws billions of money on "research" to prove it, while issuing utterly false claims, must be forced to acknowledge reality. The same applies to the energy policies on which everyone depends for electricity, a reliable supply of heating oil, and other elements of the infrastructure.

The lies must end. The end of the cooling cycle is nowhere in sight.

CHAPTER 3

Are Environmental Efforts Adequate to Meet Pollution Challenges?

Chapter Preface

Americans today generally take for granted the idea that the federal government should protect the environment, but the reality is that federal environmental legislation and regulation did not begin until the late 1960s and early 1970s. Before that time, states and localities were left to solve environmental problems without federal help. However, by mid-century, industrial activities in the United States were creating significant air and water pollution and citizens began to take notice. The result was the creation of the federal Environmental Protection Agency in 1970 and the passage of a series of US environmental laws that have helped both to clean up and prevent future environmental damage.

One of the catalysts for the US environmental movement was a book by Rachel Carson called *Silent Spring*, published in 1962. In the book, Carson railed the use of chemical pesticides and explained their detrimental effects on wildlife and the natural environment. The book was widely read and is credited with helping to inspire a ban on the chemical dichloro-diphenyl-trichloroethane, or DDT, in 1972. Several high-profile environmental disasters during this period also helped to increase public environmental awareness. One was a major oil spill by Union Oil in the ocean off Santa Barbara, California, in 1969. The incident resulted in a dump of two hundred thousand gallons of crude oil into a previously pristine ocean and coastal environment, degrading thirty-five miles of beaches and killing countless numbers of seals, dolphins, and seabirds. Another ecological disaster was Love Canal, a neighborhood of homes and a school in Niagara Falls, New York, that became famous in the 1970s as a dangerous toxic waste site. A chemical company used a landfill in this area to dispose of toxic wastes, poisoning people living nearby and causing birth defects, cancer, and other illnesses. These and other incidents shocked Americans and caused many to push their legislators for action to protect the environment.

The first national environmental legislation was the National Environmental Policy Act (NEPA), signed into law by President Richard M. Nixon on January 1, 1970, shortly after the Santa Barbara oil spill. Still in force today, NEPA requires an Environmental Impact Statement (EIS) for any federal action that could damage the environment. The EIS is used to identify and assess potential adverse effects for the environment, and to develop possible alternatives in order to spare the environment or lessen the environmental damage. In the same year as NEPA's enactment into law, President Nixon proposed the establishment of a US Environmental Protection Agency (EPA) as an independent agency in the executive branch of the federal government. On December 2, 1970, the EPA began its operations and was charged with carrying out federal laws to protect the environment. In addition, a series of other environmental laws were passed, creating a fairly comprehensive set of environmental laws and regulations. Some of the most critical ones are the Clean Air Act, the Clean Water Act, the Safe Drinking Water Act, the Resource Conservation and Recovery Act, the Toxic Substances Control Act, and the Superfund legislation.

Although federal legislation dealing with air pollution was first enacted as early as 1955, and again eight years later in 1963, the Clean Air Act of 1970 (CAA) constituted a major revision of these earlier laws. It established new nationwide standards for air quality and set new limits on pollution emissions from both stationary polluters and mobile sources like cars and trucks. Amendments in 1990 again strengthened the standards on air quality and motor vehicle emissions, as well as added regulations of toxic air pollutants, acid rain, and stratospheric ozone depletion.

The Clean Water Act (CWA), enacted in 1972, sought to protect the nation's waterways from pollution. The act established standards for discharges of industrial pollutants into navigable waters, such as streams, rivers, lakes, and oceans, with the goal of restoring and maintaining water quality so that they are fishable and swimmable. The original law did not deal with pollution caused by sources such as stormwater and agriculture runoff, but amendments passed in 1987 addressed these areas by requiring permits for industrial and municipal stormwater discharges and by funding research into agricultural pollution.

Another water pollution law, the Safe Drinking Water Act (SDWA), was passed by Congress in 1974 to protect the quality of Americans' drinking water and its sources: rivers, lakes, reservoirs, springs, and wells. Amended in 1986 and 1996, the law sets various standards for the suppliers of drinking water—physical, chemical, microbiological, and radiological—to ensure that water is purified and contaminants be kept to a minimum before it is sold to the public.

The Resource Conservation and Recovery Act/Hazardous and Solid Waste Amendments (RCRA), passed in 1976, governs the generation, transportation, treatment, storage, and disposal of hazardous waste, and also sets forth a framework for the management of nonhazardous solid wastes. The act determines what must be defined as a solid or hazardous waste and requires tracking of these materials from the time they are created to the time of their disposal, in order to make sure that they are made as safe as possible and then disposed of safely. Amendments in 1984 required phasing out land disposal of hazardous wastes, and 1986 amendments extended the law to cover environmental problems that could result from underground tanks storing petroleum and other hazardous substances.

The Toxic Substances Control Act of 1976 (TSCA), meanwhile, dealt with chemical pollutants such as polychlorinated biphenyls (PCBs), asbestos, radon, and lead-based paint. The act restricts many chemical substances and contains reporting, record-keeping, and testing requirements that track and examine about seventy-five thousand industrial chemicals that are produced or imported into the United States. The EPA has the power to ban those chemicals that it finds pose an unreasonable risk. However, the law excludes some substances, such as foods, drugs, cosmetics, and pesticides.

The Comprehensive Environmental Response, Compensation, and Liability Act, commonly known as Superfund, was a law enacted in 1980 to clean up the many abandoned hazardous waste sites throughout the country. The law established a fund (Superfund) that pays for cleaning up a list of sites (called the National Priorities List) that pose the biggest environmental threat. The money for the fund came from taxes levied on the chemical and petroleum industries. The Superfund law also details how these sites must be remediated and contains a community right-to-know provision to inform people living near Superfund locations.

There are many other valuable environmental laws, such as the Endangered Species Act of 1973, the Oil Pollution Act of 1990, and the Food Quality Protection Act of 1996, but few environmental laws have been passed in recent decades. Probably the most important area of environmental legislation currently being debated is related to reducing greenhouse gas emissions responsible for global warming. The House of Representatives approved a climate bill in 2009, but so far no such legislation has passed the Senate. The authors of viewpoints included in this chapter discuss whether the various US laws, and those of other countries, are adequate to meet today's pollution challenges.

The Barack Obama Administration Is Imposing Stricter Controls on Water Pollution

Juliet Eilperin

Juliet Eilperin, a reporter at the Washington Post *newspaper, covers national environment issues such as climate change, oceans, and air quality.*

The [Barack] Obama administration announced Wednesday [April 27, 2011] that it will impose stricter pollution controls on millions of acres of wetlands and tens of thousands of miles of streams.

The new guidelines from the Environmental Protection Agency [EPA], which will be codified in a federal regulation later this year, could prevent the dumping of mining waste and the discharge of industrial pollutants to waters that feed swimming holes and drinking water supplies. The specific restriction will depend on the waterway.

The Dispute over Clean Water Act Coverage

The question of which isolated streams and wetlands qualify for protection under the Clean Water Act has been in dispute for a decade. The Supreme Court has issued two decisions, and the George W. Bush administration issued guidance in 2003 and 2008 limiting the scope of the act.

EPA Administrator Lisa P. Jackson said in a telephone news conference with reporters that although the new rules will expand the waterways enjoying federal protection, "this is not some massive increase, as far as we can tell."

Juliet Eilperin, "EPA Proposes Stricter Controls on Water Pollution," *The Washington Post*, April 27, 2011. Used by permission of The Washington Post Writer's Group.

The policy change is likely to affect tributaries flowing into water bodies such as the Chesapeake Bay. Sen. Benjamin L. Cardin (D-Md.), who chairs the water and wildlife subcommittee of the Senate Environment and Public Works Committee, joined 13 other senators last month in urging President Obama to expand the application of federal law to such waterways.

In a statement Wednesday, Cardin said the proposed guidance "is designed to address the [Supreme] Court's concerns in a way that will protect waters that are important for fish and wildlife habitat, flood protection, and supplying drinking water. As we told the president, protecting this incredible network of waters is the first step in restoring them to health."

Once finalized, the regulations will apply federal water quality standards to a range of waterways, including the headwaters of lakes and rivers as well as intermittent streams.

Although environmentalists welcomed the decision, some groups—including livestock owners and home builders—have said it will impose an economic burden. House Republicans included a provision—subsequently dropped—in their continuing budget resolution this spring that would have blocked the EPA from instituting the rules.

"I'm disappointed that the EPA has decided to issue guidance on this contentious issue. . . . I strongly believe that it is the responsibility of Congress through the legislative process, not the EPA through guidance, to determine whether or not waters currently regulated by the states should be subject to federal jurisdiction," said Rep. Mike Simpson (R-Idaho), the chairman of the House Appropriations Committee's environment subcommittee.

Khary Cauthen, director of federal relations for the American Petroleum Institute, called the move "economically significant."

A Regulatory Mess

It remains unclear what portion of the nation's waterways will now come under stricter regulation. After the Supreme Court issued rulings that questioned whether the Clean Water Act applies to isolated streams that are not connected to navigable waterways, Bush officials said as many as 20 million acres of wetlands fell under that category.

The EPA has also abandoned more than 1,500 pollution probes in recent years, given the uncertainty surrounding what qualifies as "waters of the United States."

"It's an incredible mess," said Jon Devine, a senior attorney in the Natural Resources Defense Council's water program. He noted that just this week a federal jury in Massachusetts ruled against an individual who, without having a permit, filled in wetlands to grow cranberries, but the case dated from 1999 and could still be subject to appeal.

"It's a big deal because the resources matter," Devine said of the new guidance.

Jackson said that "we know that the current guidance is flawed. We also know that it underprotects."

The administration will take comments on its proposed guidance for 60 days, and will then proceed to draft binding rules on the matter.

The EPA Under President Barack Obama Will Regulate Greenhouse Gases

Andrew Leonard

Andrew Leonard is a senior technology writer for Salon, *an online arts, culture, and current affairs magazine.*

Never mind healthcare or bank reform. The prospect that President [Barack] Obama might gut environmental protection while eliminating unnecessary "burdensome" regulations is where some liberals get most nervous. The president put very little effort into getting any climate legislation passed, leading environmentalists to wonder: Does he actually care?

On the surface, the concern is justified. House Republicans have made the crusade to cripple the EPA's [US Environmental Protection Agency] ability to enforce limits on greenhouse gas emissions a top priority. Last week [February 2, 2011], Rep. Fred Upton, R-Mich., the chairman of the House Energy and Commerce Committee, and Sen. James Inhofe, R-Okla., announced plans to introduce legislation that would explicitly prohibit the EPA from considering "greenhouse gases" a pollutant under the terms of the Clean Air Act. Sen. Jay Rockefeller, a West Virginian Democrat, recently reintroduced a bill that would delay any EPA greenhouse gas limit enforcement for two years.

In response, the White House has been quiet. The president did not mention the words "climate change" in either his State of the Union speech or his address to the Chamber of Commerce. Quite the opposite: His only reference to the EPA at the Chamber was to cite a decision by the agency to *delay*,

Andrew Leonard, "Proof Obama Is Not Caving on Regulation: The EPA," *Salon*, February 7, 2011. This article first appeared in Salon.com, at http://www.Salon.com. An online version remains in the Salon archives. Reprinted with permission.

for three years, the setting of any limits for greenhouse gases generated from the burning of biomass, as an example of how accommodating his administration was willing to be on the regulatory front.

Greenhouse Gas Regulation Has Begun

I'm guessing Obama included that line because he or his advisers thought it would go over well with Chamber conservatives. But by pointing out an instance of EPA inaction, the president carefully avoided dwelling on the fact that the agency has *already* taken the much more significant step of beginning the process of regulating greenhouse gas emissions at power plants, oil refineries, and other *major* sources of greenhouse gas emissions. As of Jan. 2 [2011], the EPA is requiring that the operators of new, or substantially modified, facilities must get permits that will limit their future greenhouse gas emissions and require upgraded technology.

In other words, *it's already happening.* The pace is excruciatingly slow, and there are legal challenges that must be parried every step of the way, and both states and plant operators have a lot of leeway in how to deal with the proposed changes, but the machinery of greenhouse gas regulation is proceeding. And this is entirely due to the fact that the current occupant of the White House is a Democrat who appointed a strong director—Lisa Jackson—to run the EPA.

Environmentalists who want the EPA to continue [enforcing limits on greenhouse gas emissions] should be thinking hard about how to re-elect [President Barack] Obama.

[George W.] Bush's EPA refused to regulate greenhouse gases, dragging its feet even after the Supreme Court ruled, by a tight 5-4 margin, that under the terms of the Clean Air Act, greenhouse gases qualified as pollutants. The Court not only found that the EPA had the authority to regulate greenhouse gas emissions, but would be *required* to do so if the agency determined that there was scientific evidence that greenhouse gases posed a threat to public health. In November 2009, the EPA determined that greenhouse gases did pose such a threat, and the wheels went into motion.

A Political Power Play

It's worth noting how entirely contingent this entire chain of events is on raw political power. A 5-4 Supreme Court majority is a slender thread—one more George W. Bush appointee, and the decision would undoubtedly have gone the other way. Similarly, a Republican EPA would have been most unlikely to determine that greenhouse gases are a threat to public health, since the current prevailing wisdom of the Republican party is that the world is not warming because of greenhouse gas emissions.

The Republican drive to rewrite the Clean Air Act so as to make the Supreme Court's ruling irrelevant and shackle the EPA is just the latest skirmish in this primal battle, but all the hollering about job-killing regulations should not obscure the fact that the EPA is proceeding according to plan. The steady rollout of guidelines and standards will not be easy to stop. So far, the courts have generally upheld the EPA's authority— Texas is 0–3 in legal challenges—and even if Republicans do manage to get some EPA-killing legislation through the Senate, they'd still face the likelihood of a presidential veto.

Slate's tireless political reporter/blogger David Weigel had the same impression of Obama's speech to the Chamber that I did earlier today—the president made no concessions and signaled no real shift in policy. He defended his signature legislation, which the Chamber opposed, and even as he made rhetorical gestures on regulatory policy, his EPA is hard at work enforcing limits on greenhouse gas emissions. Environmentalists who want the EPA to continue doing so should be thinking hard about how to re-elect Obama, because if a Republican moves into the White House, it will all come to a screeching halt, again.

China Is Implementing an Ambitious New Environmental Plan

Deborah Seligsohn, interviewed by Bruce Gellerman

Deborah Seligsohn is the principal advisor to the China Climate and Energy Program of the World Resources Institute, a global environmental think tank. Bruce Gellerman is a host on Living on Earth, *a weekly environmental news and information program distributed by Public Radio International.*

China has released its new blueprint for the future of the country. As Deborah Seligsohn of the World Resources Institute tells Living on Earth host Bruce Gellerman the five year plan is more environmentally ambitious than anything China has proposed in the past.

Bruce Gellerman: *China's latest blueprint for the future has a distinctively green tinge. The People's Republic, already the world's second largest economy, is also the largest emitter of greenhouse gases. China's new five-year plan deals with both the environment and the economy.*

It projects the gross domestic product will rise 40 percent by 2015, while the use of energy needed to produce all that economic growth will increase by just 16 percent. Deborah Seligsohn calls that an ambitious goal. Seligsohn is a principle advisor for the World Resources Institute's China Climate and Energy Program.

Deborah Seligsohn: It's the first time they've had a major climate section in their five-year plan. The focus on environment is also much, much larger than it's ever been before.

They also announced separately from the plan that they plan to put a total cap on energy use in the country.

An energy cap?

Yes, it would limit total amount of energy use. They're going to make more stuff with less energy per unit growth. So they're going to reduce the rate of increase, and it will require them to really increase the amount of energy efficiency they do and also the amount of non-fossil fuel—hydro, wind, solar, nuclear.

Coal accounts for, what, 80 percent of China's emissions or more. How are they going to continue making more stuff and use coal and still reduce their carbon footprint?

Well, I think the percentage of coal in the mix is going to go down. They also are doing a lot to just improve the efficiency of coal, and they're trying to put use [of] some natural gas instead of coal as well. All of those reduce the amount of CO_2 [carbon dioxide] per unit of output.

Not only do [the Chinese] have the most wind power installed in the world, they're growing at the fastest rate, and they're just leaving everybody else way behind.

Well, they do have a lot of people. They have 1 and a third billion people and they all want cars—they have huge traffic jams that go on for days—how are they going to deal with that?

They may all want cars, but they're not all going to buy cars. I mean it's important to keep the vehicle numbers in perspective. In the United States, everybody in the whole country basically relies on cars. In China, it's a few big cities that operate like the US—the rest of the country is still much, much poorer. But part of this plan is an incredibly ambitious transportation plan.

They're talking about increasing their high-speed rail network so the inter-city transportation [is] several-fold, actually. And they're also talking about a massive increase in urban subway lines. So, they're trying to give people good alternatives to using their own car. And actually, the global evidence is that what controls vehicle use is simply not building the roads—building the other forms of transportation. Whether the people buy the cars or not is not as important as whether they have a place to use them.

Well, in terms of infrastructure, this past year China just surpassed the United States as the nation with the most installed wind power, but as I understand it, 30 percent of that wind power isn't plugged into the grid!

It gets plugged into the grid—they just run about a four-month lag.

Ah.

And their wind power goals for the next five years are much more ambitious. They're talking about 70 giga-watts in the next five years, which is more than double what they currently have. And so not only do they have the most wind power installed in the world, they're growing at the fastest rate, and they're just leaving everybody else way behind.

I heard they also want to go green with trees—they have a huge re-forestry program.

They've had a huge re-forestry program for the entire 60-year history of the People's Republic of China. They started in 1949 with 8.6 percent tree cover, and today it's around 20 percent. And the goal in the next plan is to get up to 21-point-something. They're also setting a forest stock volume goal to make sure that these forests are dense and healthy.

You know, Deborah, China is of course a planned economy— it's top-down, and the government can dictate what it wants to do, but are the people embracing an environmental ethic? Is environmentalism becoming part of the culture?

China is a very complicated place. I would not call it purely top-down—I think everyone who comes here feels the bottom-up ferment, especially in terms of economic activity. But, in terms of the environmental thing, what's been so interesting is that the environmental ministry has actually used public opinion very, very effectively to support its role. Realizing the public really cares about the environment—that people worry about, "what's my air like," "what's my water like"—they've used that quite assiduously. They are much more open with the public, they meet with the press, the minister of environment put a long, long very frank letter on his webpage about what China's critical environmental issues are and what needs to be done. So, this time around, they're going much more ambitious.

Well, Deborah Seligsohn, thank you very much, really appreciate it.

You're welcome!

Deborah Seligsohn is a Principal Advisor to the World Resources Institute's China Climate and Energy Program—we spoke to her in Beijing.

US Environmental Efforts Cannot Address Global Air Pollution Created by Asian Economies

David Kirby

David Kirby is an American journalist who contributes to a number of publications, including the science magazine Discover.

"There is no place called away." It is a statement worthy of [American writer] Gertrude Stein, but University of Washington atmospheric chemist Dan Jaffe says it with conviction: None of the contamination we pump into the air just disappears. It might get diluted, blended, or chemically transformed, but it has to go somewhere. And when it comes to pollutants produced by the booming economies of East Asia, that somewhere often means right here, the mainland of the United States.

Air Pollution from China

Jaffe and a new breed of global air detectives are delivering a sobering message to policy makers everywhere: Carbon dioxide, the predominant driver of global warming, is not the only industrial by-product whose effects can be felt around the world. Prevailing winds across the Pacific are pushing thousands of tons of other contaminants—including mercury, sulfates, ozone, black carbon, and desert dust—over the ocean each year. Some of this atmospheric junk settles into the cold waters of the North Pacific, but much of it eventually merges with the global air pollution pool that circumnavigates the planet.

David Kirby, "Made in China: Our Toxic, Imported Air Pollution," *Discover*, March 18, 2011. Used by permission.

These contaminants are implicated in a long list of health problems, including neurodegenerative disease, cancer, emphysema, and perhaps even pandemics like avian flu. And when wind and weather conditions are right, they reach North America within days. Dust, ozone, and carbon can accumulate in valleys and basins, and mercury can be pulled to earth through atmospheric sinks that deposit it across large swaths of land.

Pollution and production have gone hand in hand at least since the Industrial Revolution, and it is not unusual for a developing nation to value economic growth over environmental regulation. "Pollute first, clean up later" can be the general attitude, says Jennifer Turner, director of the China Environment Forum at the Woodrow Wilson International Center for Scholars. The intensity of the current change is truly new, however.

China in particular stands out because of its sudden role as the world's factory, its enormous population, and the mass migration of that population to urban centers; 350 million people, equivalent to the entire U.S. population, will be moving to its cities over the next 10 years. China now emits more mercury than the United States, India, and Europe combined. "What's different about China is the scale and speed of pollution and environmental degradation," Turner says. "It's like nothing the world has ever seen."

Development there is racing far ahead of environmental regulation. "Standards in the United States have gotten tighter because we've learned that ever-lower levels of air pollution affect health, especially in babies and the elderly," Jaffe says. As pollutants coming from Asia increase, though, it becomes harder to meet the stricter standards that our new laws impose.

The incoming pollution has sparked a fractious international debate. Officials in the United States and Europe have embraced the warnings of the soft-spoken Jaffe, who, with flecks of red and gray in his trim beard, looks every bit the part of a sober environmental watchdog. In China, where economic expansion has run at 8 to 14 percent a year since 2001, the same facts are seen through a different lens. . . .

China's smog-filled cities are ringed with heavy industry, metal smelters, and coal-fired power plants, all crucial to that fast-growing economy even as they spew tons of carbon, metals, gases, and soot into the air. China's highways are crawling with the newly acquired cars of a burgeoning middle class. Still, "it's unfair to put all the blame on China or Asia," says Xinbin Feng of the Institute of Geochemistry at the Chinese Academy of Sciences, a government-associated research facility. All regions of the world contribute pollutants, he notes. And much of the emissions are generated from making products consumed by the West.

Our economic link with China makes all the headlines, but Jaffe's work shows that we are environmentally bound to the world's fastest-rising nation as well.

Looking for Chinese Pollutants

Dan Jaffe has been worrying about air pollution since childhood. Growing up near Boston [Massachusetts], he liked to fish in local wetlands, where he first learned about acid rain. "I had a great science teacher, and we did a project in the Blue Hills area. We found that the acidity of the lake was rising," he recalls. The fledgling environmental investigator began chatting with fishermen around New England. "All these old-timers kept telling me the lakes had been full of fish that were now gone. That mobilized me to think about when we burn fossil fuels or dump garbage, there is no way it just goes somewhere else."

By 1997 Jaffe was living in Seattle [Washington], and his interest had taken a slant: Could pollution reaching his city be blowing in from somewhere else? "We had a hunch that pollutants could be carried across the ocean, and we had satellite imagery to show that," Jaffe says. "And we noticed our up-stream neighbors in Asia were developing very rapidly. I asked the question: Could we see those pollutants coming over to the United States?"

Jaffe's colleagues considered it improbable that a concentration of pollutants high enough to significantly impact American air quality could travel thousands of miles across the Pacific Ocean; they expected he would find just insignificant traces. Despite their skepticism, Jaffe set out to find the proof. First he gathered the necessary equipment. Devices to measure carbon monoxide, aerosols, sulfur dioxide, and hydrocarbons could all be bought off the shelf. He loaded the equipment into some university trucks and set out for the school's weather observatory at Cheeka Peak. The little mountain was an arduous five-hour drive northwest of Seattle, but it was also known for the cleanest air in the Northern Hemisphere. He reckoned that if he tested this reputedly pristine air when a westerly wind was blowing in from the Pacific, the Asian pollutants might show up.

The next step was identifying the true source of the pollutants. Jaffe found his answer in atmospheric circulation models, created with the help of data from Earth-imaging satellites, that allowed him to trace the pollutants' path backward in time. A paper he published two years later summarized his conclusions succinctly. The pollutants "were all statistically elevated . . . when the trajectory originated over Asia."

Mercury Pollution from China

Officials at the U.S. Environmental Protection Agency [EPA] took note, and by 1999 they were calling Jaffe to talk. They were not calling about aerosols or hydrocarbons, however, as concerning as those pollutants might be. Instead, they were interested in a pollutant that Jaffe had not looked for in his air samples: mercury.

Mercury is a common heavy metal, ubiquitous in solid material on the earth's surface. While it is trapped it is of little consequence to human health. But whenever metal is smelted or coal is burned, some mercury is released. It gets into the food chain and diffuses deep into the ocean. It eventually finds its way into fish, rice, vegetables, and fruit.

When inorganic mercury (whether from industry or nature) gets into wet soil or a waterway, sulfate-reducing bacteria begin incorporating it into an organic and far more absorbable compound called methylmercury. As microorganisms consume the methylmercury, the metal accumulates and migrates up the food chain; that is why the largest predator fish (sharks and swordfish, for example) typically have the highest concentrations. Nine-tenths of the mercury found in Americans' blood is the methyl form, and most comes from fish, especially Pacific fish. About 40 percent of all mercury exposure in the United States comes from Pacific tuna that has been touched by pollution.

In pregnant women, methylmercury can cross the placenta and negatively affect fetal brain development. Other pollutants that the fetus is exposed to can also cause toxic effects, "potentially leading to neurological, immunological, and other disorders," says Harvard epidemiologist Philippe Grandjean, a leading authority on the risks associated with chemical exposure during early development. Prenatal exposure to mercury and other pollutants can lead to lower IQ in children—even at today's lower levels, achieved in the United States after lead paint and leaded gasoline were banned. . . .

Drawing insights from [other researchers], Jaffe looked at his data anew. If mercury were arriving from China, he should be able to detect it, yet his operation on Cheeka Peak showed no such signal. Conducting reconnaissance from a plane, he realized why. The peak, at 1,500 feet, hovered below the mercury plume line. Seeking a higher perch, he chose Mount Bachelor, a ski resort in central Oregon with an altitude of 9,000 feet.

In late winter 2004, Jaffe and his students huddled deep in their down jackets, bracing against a bitter gale that buffeted the chairlift ferrying them and their costly equipment to the summit. Inside the mountaintop lodge they installed a small computer lab and extended tubes outside to vacuum up the air. Later that year they conducted a similar experiment in Okinawa, Japan.

Another Chinese import is black carbon, the soot produced by cars, stoves, factories, and crop burning and a major component of Chinese haze.

Back in Washington, they plotted their analysis of mercury in the air against satellite data showing wind currents. "My hypothesis was that we would see the same chemicals, including the same ratio of mercury to carbon monoxide, from Mount Bachelor and Japan," Jaffe says. The numbers showed exactly the expected similarity. "This was a real 'aha' moment for us, because the two regions were phenomenally close."

It was the first time anyone had decisively identified Asian mercury in American air, and the quantities were stunning. The levels Jaffe measured suggested that Asia was churning out 1,400 tons a year. The results were a shock to many scientists, Jaffe says, because "they still couldn't wrap their heads around the magnitude of the pollution and how dirty China's industry was." They were only starting to understand the global nature of the mercury problem.

Over the years, Jaffe's Mount Bachelor Observatory has also monitored many other noxious pollutants wafting across the Pacific. One major category is sulfates, associated with lung and heart disease. When sulfur dioxide exits China's coal and oil smokestacks, it converts into sulfates in the air. "Sulfates are water-soluble and get removed from the atmosphere relatively quickly, creating acid rain that falls in China, Korea, and Japan," Jaffe says. Yet some of the sulfates stay aloft, finding their way here and contributing to smog along the West Coast.

Perhaps the most counterintuitive traveling contaminant is ozone, commonly associated with ground-level pollution in cities.

Other Chinese Pollutants

Another Chinese import is black carbon, the soot produced by cars, stoves, factories, and crop burning and a major component of Chinese haze. The small diameter of the carbon particles means they can penetrate deep inside the lungs, providing absorption sites for secondary toxins that would otherwise be cleared. This compounds the danger, making black carbon an especially potent risk factor for lung disease and premature death.

The biggest pollutant coming out of Asia, at least in terms of sheer mass, could be dust from the region's swelling deserts. "It's not a new phenomenon," Jaffe says, but it has gotten worse with deforestation and desertification caused by poorly managed agriculture. About every three years, a huge dust storm over China sends enormous clouds across the Pacific. "We can visually see it," Jaffe says. "It usually hangs around for about a week. We've tried to quantify how much it contributes to the particulate loading here, and it's a little under 10 percent of the U.S. standard on average each year. It's a significant amount."

Chinese dust has obscured vistas in U.S. national parks, even on the East Coast. The amount of dust is widely variable and can hit rare extreme peaks. The highest level recorded was from a 2001 dust event. "It reached approximately two-thirds of the U.S. air quality standard at several sites along the West Coast," he reports. One study from Taiwan tracked avian flu outbreaks downwind of Asian dust storms and found that the flu virus might be transported long-distance by air spiked with the dust.

Perhaps the most counterintuitive traveling contaminant is ozone, commonly associated with ground-level pollution in cities. Volatile organic compounds, carbon monoxide, and nitrogen oxides from Asian cars and industry mix in the atmosphere as they cross the Pacific Ocean and convert in sunlight into ozone, a main ingredient in smog, Jaffe explains. When air with high ozone concentrations touches down in North America, it can pose the classic dangers of urban smog: heart disease, lung disease, and death.

Jaffe recently coauthored a paper on Asian ozone coming to America. It found that ozone levels above western North America creep upward every spring. "When air was coming from Asia, the trend was strongest. That was the nail in the coffin," Jaffe says. "The increase was estimated at 0.5 part per billion [ppb] per year. But that's huge. In 10 years that's another 5 ppb. Let's say the EPA orders a 5 ppb reduction and we achieve that, and yet, because of the growing global pool, in 10 years that gets wiped out. We'll have to keep reducing our emissions just to stay even.". . .

A Global Problem

The underlying message of Jaffe's detective work should not be all that surprising: All of the world's atmosphere is interconnected. People have accepted this notion when it comes to carbon dioxide or the chemicals that eat away at the ozone layer, but Jaffe is finding that they are still coming to terms with the reality that it applies to industrial pollutants in general.

The fact is, those pollutants are everybody's responsibility, not just China's. The EPA has estimated that just one-quarter of U.S. mercury emissions from coal-burning power plants are deposited within the contiguous U.S. The remainder enters the global cycle. Conversely, current estimates are that less than half of all mercury deposition within the United States comes from American sources.

Then again, the United States has spent considerable effort over the past half-century trying to clean up its act. China is still much more focused on production. To fuel its boom, China has become a pioneer in wind power but has also begun buying up huge inventories of coal from markets around the world. [Argonne National Laboratory scientist David] Streets recently estimated that China's use of coal for electricity generation will rise nearly 40 percent over the next decade, from 1.29 billion tons last year to 1.77 billion tons in 2020. That is a lot more pollution to come.

"It's a classic example of a tragedy of the commons," Jaffe says, referring to a dilemma in which individuals act in their own self-interest and deplete a shared resource. "If 20 people are fishing in the same pond, with no fishing limit, then you catch as many as you can because it will be empty in weeks. Nobody has an incentive to conserve, and the same goes for pollution."

The discovery of the global mercury cycle underscores the need for an international treaty to address such pollutants. Under the auspices of the United Nations [UN], negotiations have at least begun. Jaffe, Streets, and China's Xinbin Feng are now consultants to the U.N. Environment Programme's Global Partnership on Mercury Atmospheric Transport and Fate Research, which helped contribute data that led to a proposed U.N. mercury treaty in 2009.

When it comes to some pollutants, China has taken important steps. For instance, recent policies encourage desulfurization and other filtering technology in power plants. But convincing developing nations to move aggressively on mercury may be at least as tough as mobilizing them against carbon emissions. "This is not considered a pollutant that urgently needs to be controlled on the national level," Feng says.

"It's not fair that you emitted so much mercury and other pollutants when you had the chance to industrialize. You had 200 years, and now you want to stop other countries from developing too."

"We need to be concerned," Jaffe counters in his low-key way. "There is no Planet B. We all live downwind."

China's Fight Against Pollution Is Faltering

David Stanway

David Stanway is a reporter for Thompson Reuters, an international news service.

China's fight against chronic pollution is faltering in the face of urbanization and rapid growth, though the last five years have seen some progress, the country's environment ministry said on Saturday [March 2011].

China was still producing more "traditional pollutants" than it could bear, but new industries were also creating torrents of dangerous chemicals and mountains of electronic waste, said Zhang Lijun, vice-minister of environmental protection.

"We're still a developing country—the standard of living is still not high, employment trends are serious and each level of government is paying attention to economic growth," he said.

China's consumption of coal—the dirtiest of fossil fuels and a major source of acid rain, water pollution and climate change—rose around 1 billion tons in the five years from 2006, and could rise another billion in the next five, he said.

"In this kind of territory, if we add emissions from another 1 billion tons of coal, how big will the impact be on our environment?" Zhang told reporters.

Tackling Carbon

China plans to cut its levels of carbon intensity—the amount of carbon dioxide produced per unit of GDP [gross domestic product]—by 17 percent by the end of 2015. Zhang said individual regions had already been set targets.

David Stanway, "China Says Environment Still Suffering Growth Pain," *Planet Ark*, March 14, 2011. Used by permission.

China's climate change measures have normally been the responsibility of the growth-focused National Development and Reform Commission [NDRC], with the environment ministry taking on more immediate threats such as acid rain-inducing sulphur dioxide and nitrogen oxides, as well as water and soil contamination.

China will continue to give priority to economic growth, especially in poorer regions.

But environment minister Zhou Shengxian said last month the ministry would include CO_2 [carbon dioxide] emissions in the environmental impact assessments of major projects.

Zhang said the ministry would only approve individual projects that fit in with regional greenhouse gas targets, and the NDRC would still play the leading role in China's climate change efforts.

Growth vs. Pollution

The ministry was upgraded from a lower-level "bureau" just three years ago, and fears remain that China will continue to give priority to economic growth, especially in poorer regions.

The ministry has not been involved in climate change discussions, and environmental activists say it has been frozen out of policy debates about the development of hydropower—seen as a key part of China's "low-carbon" strategy over the next decade.

Zhang said it would be "very easy" to sacrifice the economy for the environment, but the crucial issue for local governments was greener growth, and China already had systems to ensure regions meet their duty to both create jobs and protect health.

China aims to keep annual growth at around 7 percent in the next five years, but Zhao Hualin, head of the ministry's pollution control office, told reporters the GDP target was only for "guidance" and would not supersede environmental goals.

China will publish its detailed "five-year plan" for the environment after it has been approved by the State Council, the country's cabinet. It has already announced that sulphur dioxide and chemical oxygen demand will be cut by a further 8 percent in the next five years, and nitrogen oxide and ammonium nitrate will also be cut by 8 to 10 percent.

Zhang said nitrogen oxide represented the biggest challenge, and China should consider imposing car ownership curbs in its largest cities and also cap coal consumption in built-up regions such as the Pearl and Yangtze river deltas.

Responding to the closure of three nuclear power plants in Japan following the country's biggest ever earthquake on Friday, Zhang said Beijing would keep a close eye on the situation.

"We have already begun monitoring coastal cities to test whether Japan's nuclear leaks will affect China but up to now everything is normal."

He said radioactive emissions standards around China's 13 existing reactors were actually higher than international norms.

Corporate Polluters Are Not Required to Pay for the Pollution They Cause

Juliette Jowit

Juliette Jowit is the environment editor for the Observer, *a British newspaper.*

The cost of pollution and other damage to the natural environment caused by the world's biggest companies would wipe out more than one-third of their profits if they were held financially accountable, a major unpublished study for the United Nations [UN] has found.

The report comes amid growing concern that no one is made to pay for most of the use, loss and damage of the environment, which is reaching crisis proportions in the form of pollution and the rapid loss of freshwater, fisheries and fertile soils.

Environmental Damage Worth Trillions of Dollars

Later this year [2010], another huge UN study—dubbed the "Stern for nature" after the influential report on the economics of climate change by Sir Nicholas Stern—will attempt to put a price on such global environmental damage, and suggest ways to prevent it. The report, led by economist Pavan Sukhdev, is likely to argue for abolition of billions of dollars of subsidies to harmful industries like agriculture, energy and transport, tougher regulations and more taxes on companies that cause the damage.

Ahead of changes which would have a profound effect—not just on companies' profits but also their customers and pension funds and other investors—the UN-backed Principles for Responsible Investment initiative and the United Nations Environment Programme jointly ordered a report into the activities of the 3,000 biggest public companies in the world, which includes household names from the UK's [United Kingdom's] FTSE 100 [share index of the hundred most highly-capitalized companies listed on the London Stock Exchange] and other major stockmarkets.

The study, conducted by London-based consultancy Trucost and due to be published this summer, found the estimated combined damage was worth US$2.2 trillion (£1.4tn [trillion]) in 2008—a figure bigger than the national economies of all but seven countries in the world that year.

The figure equates to 6–7% of the companies' combined turnover, or an average of one-third of their profits, though some businesses would be much harder hit than others.

"What we're talking about is a completely new paradigm," said Richard Mattison, Trucost's chief operating officer and leader of the report team. "Externalities of this scale and nature pose a major risk to the global economy and markets are not fully aware of these risks, nor do they know how to deal with them."

The biggest single impact on the $2.2tn estimate, accounting for more than half of the total, was emissions of greenhouse gases blamed for climate change. Other major "costs" were local air pollution such as particulates, and the damage caused by the over-use and pollution of freshwater.

The true figure is likely to be even higher because the $2.2tn does not include damage caused by household and government consumption of goods and services, such as energy used to power appliances or waste; the "social impacts" such as the migration of people driven out of affected areas, or the long-term effects of any damage other than that from climate change. The final report will also include a higher total estimate which includes those long-term effects of problems such as toxic waste.

Making Polluters Pay

Trucost did not want to comment before the final report on which sectors incurred the highest "costs" of environmental damage, but they are likely to include power companies and heavy energy users like aluminium producers because of the greenhouse gases that result from burning fossil fuels. Heavy water users like food, drink and clothing companies are also likely to feature high up on the list.

Continued inefficient use of natural resources will cause significant impacts on [national economies] overall, and a massive problem for governments to fix.

Sukhdev said the heads of the major companies at this year's annual economic summit in Davos, Switzerland, were increasingly concerned about the impact on their business if they were stopped or forced to pay for the damage.

"It can make the difference between profit and loss," Sukhdev told the annual Earthwatch Oxford lecture last week. "That sense of foreboding is there with many, many [chief executives], and that potential is a good thing because it leads to solutions."

The aim of the study is to encourage and help investors lobby companies to reduce their environmental impact before concerned governments act to restrict them through taxes or regulations, said Mattison.

"It's going to be a significant proportion of a lot of companies' profit margins," Mattison told the *Guardian*. "Whether they actually have to pay for these costs will be determined by the appetite for policy makers to enforce the 'polluter pays' principle. We should be seeking ways to fix the system, rather than waiting for the economy to adapt. Continued inefficient use of natural resources will cause significant impacts on [national economies] overall, and a massive problem for governments to fix."

Another major concern is the risk that companies simply run out of resources they need to operate, said Andrea Moffat, of the US-based investor lobby group Ceres, whose members include more than 80 funds with assets worth more than US$8tn. An example was the estimated loss of 20,000 jobs and $1bn [billion] last year for agricultural companies because of water shortages in California, said Moffat.

CHAPTER 4

What Are the Emerging Solutions to Environmental Pollution?

Chapter Preface

It is an undisputed fact that today's world runs on fossil fuels—oil, natural gas, and coal. These fuels power the world economy and are essential to providing the products and technologies that have become synonymous with modern lifestyles. In fact, oil is key to almost every part of the US and the global economy, including sectors from agriculture and food production to most types of manufacturing, the drug industry, airlines and other types of transportation, and the military. Scientists warn, however, that this fossil fuel dependence is producing carbon dioxide and other greenhouse gas emissions that are warming the world's climate in potentially catastrophic ways. At the same time, energy experts claim that we may soon reach a point of peak oil, after which oil supplies will rapidly decline and oil prices will skyrocket. The obvious solution to both these problems, many people agree, is to reduce our dependence on fossil fuels and move towards alternative energy sources that produce low or zero greenhouse emissions. However, proponents of this strategy of embracing "green energy" sources, such as solar, wind, and geothermal, face many obstacles.

The global fossil fuel dependence developed during the Industrial Revolution, a period of economic development that radically changed the way humans work and live. Beginning in the early 1700s, machinery slowly replaced manual labor and animal power, and fossil fuels replaced early energy sources of wind, water, and wood. In addition, new industrial machines, such as the steam engine, were invented to make the production of goods both easier and faster. Steam engines ran on coal but with the dawn of the oil era in the late 1800s and early 1900s and the invention of the automobile, oil replaced coal as the standard fuel for transportation, while coal and natural gas became the main energy sources for heating homes and producing electricity.

Two centuries of fossil fuel usage, however, appear to be threatening the Earth's environment in potentially devastating ways. Although some scientists and critics still dispute the idea that human greenhouse gas emissions are causing the climate to warm, the majority of the world's scientists and climate experts believe that human-induced global warming is clearly happening. In 2007, for example, the Intergovernmental Panel on Climate Change (IPCC), a scientific body charged by the United Nations with summarizing the best climate science, concluded that evidence of climate warming is unequivocal. According to this report, global greenhouse gas emissions have dramatically increased during the industrial period and this increase is very likely due to human activities, such as the burning of fossil fuels. The IPCC found that effects of this global warming—more frequent heat waves, heavy precipitation, drought, melting of glaciers and sea ice, and increasing average sea levels—are already apparent. This warming trend is expected to continue, and the IPCC warns that if humans do not make significant reductions in emissions in the near future, the results could be irreversible. The worst case consequences could include the loss of many animal and plant species, degradation of fisheries and land ecosystems, and loss of water resources—environmental damage that could jeopardize global food production, cause water shortages, threaten human health, and create huge economic and social upheavals around the world.

Yet the global addiction to fossil fuels makes solving global warming very difficult. Many climate experts have urged policymakers to stabilize greenhouse gas concentrations in the atmosphere at a level that would keep average global temperatures at no more than 2 degrees Celsius (3.6 degrees Fahrenheit) above preindustrial levels. This, experts say, would avoid some of the worst, most irreversible consequences of climate change. Other scientists argue that much deeper emission cuts are necessary. Even the most moderate goals will be difficult to reach, however, because they essentially involve transforming global energy usage.

Most of the solutions being proposed involve cutting fossil fuel consumption and moving toward so-called green energy sources that emit fewer or zero emissions. Efforts to reduce global emissions have employed international carbon caps—a system created by a 1997 international treaty called the Kyoto Protocol that sets an overall limit on the amount of allowable carbon emissions and allows for carbon trading among countries. Although this effort has produced some success, it has not been enough to slow global emissions substantially. As a result, many experts are putting their faith in the green energy movement as the only real solution to climate change. These experts argue that a clean energy future must be created by major investments in new environmentally friendly, renewable technologies—solar, wind, geothermal, hydropower, biofuels, hydrogen, and lithium batteries, to name a few. Advancements of these technologies, proponents claim, could solve global warming by transforming energy usage around the world.

The main problem with green energy, however, is that no single clean energy source appears capable of replacing cheap fossil fuels. Rather, energy experts think that it will take many different kinds of alternative fuels as well as improvements in energy efficiency and vehicle fuel economy to make up for the loss of fossil energy sources. Some energy researchers also propose that the world must consider bridge strategies that would allow people and industries to be weaned slowly off of the dirtiest fossil fuels—coal and oil—by relying temporarily on less-polluting natural gas and other options like nuclear power. Because there is no obvious, global, green strategy, each country is left to devise its own solutions. The result is that some countries, such as Germany and China, have become leaders in this arena, investing large amounts of their budgets in new green technologies, while others, such as the United States, have been more reluctant to embrace alternative fuels. The viewpoints in this chapter address some of the problems caused by fossil fuel usage and propose solutions to this and other environmental ills.

American Rivers Must Be Protected from Fracking and Other Threats

Mark Clayton

Mark Clayton is a staff writer for the Christian Science Monitor, *an international news organization.*

After decades of declining US natural-gas production, an advanced drilling system so powerful it fractures rock with high-pressure fluid is opening up vast shale-gas deposits.

Hydraulic Fracturing

Instead of falling, US gas production is rising, with up to 118 years' worth of "unconventional" natural gas reserves in 21 huge shale basins, an industry study in July [2008] reported. Such reserves could make the nation more energy self-sufficient and provide more of a cleaner "bridge fuel" to help meet carbon-reduction goals urged by environmentalists.

Shale gas reserves have a powerful economic lure. Companies, states, and landowners could all reap a windfall in the tens of billions. Some also predict lower heating costs for residential gas users as production increases.

Now, scores of natural gas companies are fanning out from Fort Worth, Texas, where hydraulic fracturing of shale has been done for at least five years, to lease shale lands in 19 states, including Pennsylvania and New York.

But some warn that by expanding "hydraulic fracturing" of shale, America strikes a Faustian bargain: It gains new energy reserves, but it consumes and quite possibly pollutes critical water resources.

Mark Clayton, "Controversial Path to Possible Glut of Natural Gas," *Christian Science Monitor*, September 17, 2008. Used by permission of Christian Science Monitor.

"People need to understand that these are not your old-fashioned gas wells," says Tracy Carluccio, special projects director for Delaware Riverkeeper, a watchdog group worried about a surge in new gas drilling from New York to Pennsylvania and from Ohio to West Virginia. "This technology produces tremendous amounts of polluted water and uses dangerous chemicals in every single well that's developed."

Traditional gas wells bore straight into porous stone, using a few thousand gallons of water during drilling. But dense shale has gas locked inside.

Hydraulic fracturing, or "fracking," and horizontal drilling unlock it.

Fracking Pollutes Water Resources

Each hydraulically fractured horizontal well can require from 2 million to 7 million gallons of fresh water mixed with sand and thousands of gallons of industrial chemicals to make the water penetrate more easily.

This frac-water mixture is blasted at high pressure into shale deposits up to 10,000 feet deep, fracturing them. The sand lodges in the cracks, propping them open and providing a path for the gas to exit after external pressure is released.

Besides using vast amounts of groundwater, scientists and environmentalists worry that toxic frac water—30 percent or more—remains underground and may years later pollute freshwater aquifers.

Millions of gallons of frac water come back to the surface. It could be treated, but in Texas it is most often reinjected into the ground.

Millions more gallons of "produced" water flow out later during gas production. This flow, too, is often tainted with radioactivity and poisons from the shale. Often stored in pits, that waste can leak or overflow while awaiting reinjection.

Simply put: "Each of these wells uses millions of gallons of fresh water, and all of it is going to be contaminated," Ms. Carluccio says. Industry spokesmen say such fears are over-blown.

"The wells we drill . . . are insulated with concrete," says Chip Minty, a spokesman for Devon Energy, an Oklahoma City-based gas company that pioneered hydraulic fracturing in the Barnett shale formation beneath Fort Worth, Texas. "The purpose is to protect any kind of aquifer or ground water layer. Those processes are controlled by regulatory agencies, and that keeps us safe from any kind of aquifer pollution."

A pioneer in "best practices," Devon has also developed a way to purify and reuse frac water. But those techniques are costly and not widely used at present. Whether such practices will be required elsewhere is an open question.

Is New York City's Drinking Water At Risk?

In July, New York's governor signed a bill to expand shale-gas drilling using fracturing technology, which could bring the state $1 billion in annual revenues. But the state is first requiring an updated environmental assessment and may yet require companies to reveal the type of chemicals they mix with the water they shoot down the wells—something that Texas does not require.

New York City is one of only four large cities in the nation with unfiltered drinking water. It flows from the northern Catskill region. That's the same basin in which gas companies want to drill.

Drilling "is completely and utterly inconsistent with a drinking water supply," said New York City Councilman James Gennaro at a press conference last month. "This would destroy the New York City watershed, and for what? For short-term gains on natural gas."

But while New York has a drilling freeze pending its environmental review, a gas-drilling rush is on in Pennsylvania's Susquehanna River region. Scores of wells are being drilled, with applications pending to drill hundreds more. In the long run, some say there may be 10,000 new gas wells across the region.

"We're hearing various stories ... about flow backwater," says Susan Obleski, a spokeswoman for the Susquehanna River Basin Commission [SRBC], which oversees water usage. "We could eventually be seeing 29 million gallons a day usage by this industry. That sounds like a lot, but golf courses use double that."

The concern, however, is that the most productive gas drilling areas tend to be in remote, forested areas, with forested streams—headwaters areas. If water is removed in significant amounts from there, it could damage ecosystems and Susquehanna watershed water quality.

The SRBC has issued two cease-and-desist orders to companies illegally removing water. It has told 23 others to clarify requirements, and found that about 50, in all, are vying for water, leases, and drilling permits in the region.

The Energy Policy Act of 2005 exempts companies from being forced by the Clean Water Act, Safe Drinking Water Act, and other federal laws to reveal what chemicals are in their fracturing fluids.

What's Being Injected Deep Underground?

Hydraulic fracturing and horizontal drilling are not new. Both date back decades. But their combined use to get gas from shale formations is new within the past decade.

Hydraulic fracturing has long been used to get gas from coal beds, a process some say is similar to shale-gas fracturing.

An Environmental Protection Agency [EPA] study in 2004 concluded that hydraulic fracturing to get methane gas from coal beds "poses little or no threat" to drinking water supplies. But several EPA scientists have challenged that finding.

"EPA produced a final report ... that I believe is scientifically unsound and contrary to the purposes of law," Weston Wilson, a 30–year EPA veteran, wrote in a whistle-blower petition in 2004. "Based on the available science and literature, EPA's conclusions are unsupportable."

Today, chemicals used in fracturing are considered by the companies to be trade secrets. The Energy Policy Act of 2005 exempts companies from being forced by the Clean Water Act, Safe Drinking Water Act, and other federal laws to reveal what chemicals are in their fracturing fluids.

But some say that it's critical to know what's being injected deep underground.

"We're very concerned about this toxic drilling and hydraulic fracturing," says Gwen Lachelt, director of the Oil and Gas Accountability Project in Durango, Colo. "We need to know what's in what they're putting into the ground."

Human Interactions with the Ocean Must Quickly Become More Sustainable

A.D. Rogers and D.d'A. Laffoley

A.D. Rogers is scientific director of the International Programme on the State of the Ocean (IPSO), an organization that seeks to improve the way the ocean is managed and protected, and a professor in the Department of Zoology at University of Oxford in the United Kingdom. D.d'A. Laffoley is senior advisor at the International Union for Conservation of Nature (IUCN), a Swiss environmental organization.

Between 11th and 13th April 2011 world experts on the ocean met at the Margaret Thatcher Conference Centre, Somerville College, University of Oxford [United Kingdom]. This event was led by the International Programme on the State of the Ocean (IPSO), in partnership with the International Union for Conservation of Nature (IUCN), and brought together a select group of world science leaders on ocean stresses and impacts to reflect on these, and propose creative solutions.

The workshop provided a rare opportunity to interact with other disciplines to determine the net effect of what is already happening to the ocean and is projected to do so in the future. Over the three days, 27 participants from 18 organisations in 6 countries assessed the latest information on impacts and stresses, and the synergistic effects these are having on the global ocean.

Through presentations, discussions and recommendations the workshop documented and described the cumulative ef-

A.D. Rogers and D.d'A. Laffoley, "International Earth System Expert Workshop on Ocean Stresses and Impacts, Summary Report," International Programme on the State of the Ocean. Used by permission.

fects of such impacts, how these commonly act in a negatively synergistic way, and why therefore concerted action is now needed to address the consequences set out in this report. . . .

The ocean is the largest ecosystem on Earth, supports us and maintains our world in a habitable condition.

Workshop Objectives

The objectives of the workshop were to:

- Review the latest information on ocean stresses and impacts and the levels of confidence around what is being expressed;

- Summarise the likely consequence of existing stresses on the ocean;

- Summarise the likely consequence of projected stresses from 2020 through to 2050;

- Determine the synergistic effects of multiple stresses on the ocean and what this may mean for the future.

The timeline for consideration was from today through 2020 to 2050.

The workshop enabled leading experts to take a global view on how all the different effects we are having on the ocean are compromising its ability to support us. This examination of synergistic threats leads to the conclusion that we have underestimated the overall risks and that the whole of marine degradation is greater than the sum of its parts, and that degradation is now happening at a faster rate than predicted.

Oceans in Trouble

It is clear that the traditional economic and consumer values that formerly served society well, when coupled with current rates of population increase, are not sustainable. The ocean is the largest ecosystem on Earth, supports us and maintains our world in a habitable condition. To maintain the goods and services it has provided to humankind for millennia demands change in how we view, manage, govern and use marine ecosystems. The scale of the stresses on the ocean means that deferring action will increase costs in the future leading to even greater losses of benefits.

The speeds of many negative changes to the ocean are near to or are tracking the worst-case scenarios from IPCC [Intergovernmental Panel on Climate Change] and other predictions.

The key points needed to drive a common sense rethink are:

Human actions have resulted in warming and acidification of the oceans and are now causing increased hypoxia.

Studies of the Earth's past indicate that these are three symptoms that indicate disturbances of the carbon cycle associated with each of the previous five mass extinctions on Earth.

The speeds of many negative changes to the ocean are near to or are tracking the worst-case scenarios from IPCC [Intergovernmental Panel on Climate Change] and other predictions. Some are as predicted, but many are faster than anticipated, and many are still accelerating.

Consequences of current rates of change already matching those predicted under the "worst case scenario" include: the rate of decrease in Arctic Sea Ice and in the accelerated melting of both the Greenland icesheet and Antarctic ice sheets; sea level rise; and release of trapped methane from the seabed; although not yet globally significant.

The 'worst case' effects are compounding other changes more consistent with predictions including: changes in the distribution and abundance of marine species; changes in primary production; changes in the distribution of harmful algal blooms; increases in health hazards in the oceans; and loss of both large, long-lived and small fish species causing widespread impacts on marine ecosystems, including direct impacts on predator and prey species, the simplification and destabilization of food webs, reduction of resilience to the effects of climate change.

The magnitude of the cumulative impacts on the ocean is greater than previously understood

Interactions between different impacts can be negatively synergistic (negative impact greater than sum of individual stressors) or they can be antagonistic (lowering the effects of individual impacts). Examples of such interactions include: combinations of overfishing, physical disturbance, climate change effects, nutrient runoff and introductions of non-native species leading to explosions of these invasive species, including harmful algal blooms, and dead zones; increased temperature and acidification increasing the susceptibility of corals to bleaching and acting synergistically to impact the reproduction and development of other marine invertebrates; changes in the behavior, fate and toxicity of heavy metals with acidification; acidification may reduce the limiting effect of iron availability on primary production in some parts of the ocean; increased uptake of plastics by fauna and increased bioavailability of pollutants through adsorption onto the surface of microplastic particles; and feedbacks of climate change impacts on the oceans (temperature rise, sea level rise, loss of ice cover, acidification, increased storm intensity, methane release) on their rate of CO_2 [carbon dioxide] uptake and global warming.

Timelines for action are shrinking.

The longer the delay in reducing emissions the higher the annual reduction rate will have to be and the greater the financial cost. Delays will mean increased environmental damage with greater socioeconomic impacts and costs of mitigation and adaptation measures.

Resilience of the ocean to climate change impacts is severely compromised by the other stressors from human activities, including fisheries, pollution and habitat destruction.

Examples include the overfishing of reef grazers, nutrient runoff, and other forms of pollution (presence of pathogens or endocrine disrupting chemicals) reducing the recovery ability of reefs from temperature-induced mass coral bleaching. These multiple stressors promote the phase shift of reef ecosystems from being coral-dominated to algal dominated. The loss of genetic diversity from overfishing reduces ability to adapt to stressors.

Unless action is taken now, the consequences of our activities are at a high risk of causing . . . the next globally significant extinction event in the ocean.

Ecosystem collapse is occurring as a result of both current and emerging stressors.

Stressors include chemical pollutants, agriculture run-off, sediment loads and over-extraction of many components of food webs which singly and together severely impair the functioning of ecosystems. Consequences include the potential increase of harmful algal blooms in recent decades; the spread of oxygen depleted or dead zones, the disturbance of the structure and functioning of marine food webs, to the benefit of planktonic organisms of low nutritional value, such as jellyfish or other gelatinous-like organisms; dramatic changes in the microbial communities with negative impacts at the ecosystem scale; and the impact of emerging chemical contaminants in ecosystems. This impairment damages or eliminates the ability of ecosystems to support humans.

The extinction threat to marine species is rapidly increasing.

The main causes of extinctions of marine species to date are overexploitation and habitat loss. However climate change is increasingly adding to this, as evidenced by the recent assessments of reef-forming corals. Some other species ranges have already extended or shifted pole-wards and into deeper cooler waters; this may not be possible for some species to achieve, potentially leading to reduced habitats and more extinctions. Shifts in currents and temperatures will affect the food supply of animals, including at critical early stages, potentially testing their ability to survive.

The participants concluded that not only are we already experiencing severe declines in many species to the point of commercial extinction in some cases, and an unparalleled rate of regional extinctions of habitat types (e.g. mangroves and seagrass meadows), but we now face losing marine species and entire marine ecosystems, such as coral reefs, within a single generation. Unless action is taken now, the consequences of our activities are at a high risk of causing, through the combined effects of climate change, overexploitation, pollution and habitat loss, the next globally significant extinction event in the ocean. It is notable that the occurrence of multiple high intensity stressors has been a pre-requisite for all the five global extinction events of the past 600 million years.

The continued expansion in global population exerts ever increasing pressures on scarcer ocean resources.

Recommendations from the Workshop

The participants of the meeting agreed to the following recommendations based on workshop conclusions.

Technical means to achieve the solutions to many of these problems already exist, but that current societal values prevent humankind from addressing them effectively. Overcoming these barriers is core to the fundamental changes needed to achieve a sustainable and equitable future for the generations to come and which preserves the natural ecosystems of the Earth that we benefit from and enjoy today. This meeting of experts offers the following recommendations to citizens and governments everywhere to transform how we manage, govern and protect the ocean:

- *Immediate reduction in CO_2 emissions* coupled with significantly increased measures for mitigation of atmospheric CO_2 and to better manage coastal and marine carbon sinks to avoid additional emissions of greenhouse gases.

    It is a matter of urgency that the ocean is considered as a priority in the deliberations of the IPCC and UNFCCC [United Nations Framework Convention on Climate Change].

- *Urgent actions to restore the structure and function of marine ecosystems*, including the coordinated and concerted action in national waters and on the High Seas (the high seas water column and seabed area beyond national jurisdiction) by states and regional bodies to:

    reduce fishing effort to levels commensurate with long-term sustainability of fisheries and the marine environment;

    close fisheries that are not demonstrably managed following sustainable principles, or which depend wholly on government subsidies;

    establish a globally comprehensive and representative system of marine protected areas to conserve biodiversity, to build resilience, and to ensure ecologically sustainable fisheries with minimal ecological footprint;

prevent, reduce and strictly control inputs of substances that are harmful or toxic to marine organisms into the marine environment;

prevent, reduce and strictly control nutrient inputs into the marine environment through better land & river catchment management and sewage treatment;

avoid, reduce or at minimum, universally and stringently regulate oil, gas, aggregate and mineral extraction;

assess, monitor and control other uses of the marine environment such as renewable energy schemes or cable/pipeline installation through comprehensive spatial planning and impact assessments procedures.

- *Proper and universal implementation of the precautionary principle* by reversing the burden of proof so activities proceed only if they are shown not to harm the ocean singly or in combination with other activities.

- *Urgent introduction by the UN [United Nations] Security Council and the UN General Assembly of effective governance of the High Seas* beyond the jurisdiction of any individual nations. This should include a global body empowered to ensure compliance with the UN Convention on the Law of the Sea and other relevant legal duties and norms and to establish new rules, regulations and procedures where necessary to implement these requirements in an ecosystem-based and precautionary manner.

Humans Must Change Their Use of the Oceans

The current inadequate approaches to management of activities that impact the ocean have lead to intense multiple stressors acting together in many marine ecosystems.

The impact of such stressors is often negatively synergistic meaning that the combination of the two magnifies the negative impacts of each one occurring alone. This is already resulting in large-scale changes in the ocean at an increasing rate and in some regions has resulted in ecosystem collapse. The continued expansion in global population exerts ever increasing pressures on scarcer ocean resources and tackling this issue needs to be a part of the solution to current concerns.

> *Human interactions with the ocean must change with the rapid adoption of a holistic approach to sustainable management of all activities that impinge marine ecosystems.*

The changes in the ocean that are coming about as a result of human CO_2 emissions are perhaps the most significant to the Earth system particularly as they involve many feedbacks that will accelerate climate change.

The resilience of many marine ecosystems has been eroded as a result of existing stressors, leading to increased vulnerability to climate change impacts and a decreased capacity for recovery. An example is coral reefs, the most biodiverse marine ecosystem and one of the most valuable in socioeconomic terms to humankind.

Human interactions with the ocean must change with the rapid adoption of a holistic approach to sustainable management of all activities that impinge marine ecosystems. This has to be part of a wider re-evaluation of the core values of human society and its relationship to the natural world and the resources on which we all rely. As such the current and future state of the ocean should form an integral part of the discussions on sustainable development at the Earth Summit in Rio [Rio de Janeiro, Brazil], 2012.

A Clean Energy Standard Is an Essential First Step Toward a Clean Energy Future

Richard W. Caperton, Kate Gordon, Bracken Hendricks, and Daniel J. Weiss

Richard W. Caperton is a senior policy analyst, Kate Gordon is vice president for energy policy, and Bracken Hendricks and Daniel J. Weiss are senior fellows at the Center for American Progress, a progressive think tank.

The United States is at risk of being left in the dust in the clean energy race. But we can catch up. A Clean Energy Standard, or CES, which mandates that electric utilities generate a certain percentage of their power from clean energy sources, is an essential first step.

The Clean Energy Leaders

The global market for efficient and renewable energy technologies is expected to reach at least $2 trillion by the end of this decade. China and the European Union, and especially Germany, are clamoring to lead this clean energy race. These countries have set clear goals for renewable energy and energy efficiency use, along with carbon emission targets and investment strategies to promote clean technology development for export markets.

China, for instance, just released its 12th five-year plan, which mandates massive deployment of solar power in villages, a 17 percent reduction in greenhouse gas intensity, and a 16 percent reduction in the energy intensity of their economy. China also invests an estimated $12 billion per month into its clean tech sector.

Richard W. Caperton, Kate Gordon, Bracken Hendricks, and Daniel J. Weiss, "How to Shape the Clean Energy Future of the United States: CAP's Response to the 'White Paper on a Clean Energy Standard,'" Center for American Progress, April 25, 2011. Used by permission.

With the right policy tools we have the innovative strength and drive to lead the clean energy future. To do so we must increase market demand for clean energy products, help move public and private financing into clean tech industries, and create the necessary infrastructure to move these new energy resources to market.

CES is an incredibly powerful tool to boost domestic demand for clean energy products.

CES a Powerful Tool

Countries abroad—and states within our own nation—that have adopted renewable or clean energy standards demonstrate that a CES is an incredibly powerful tool to boost domestic demand for clean energy products. This in turn provides certainty for those who invent, manufacture, and install those products, and helps to grow a strong national clean energy industry.

President Barack Obama put a CES proposal on the table in his most recent State of the Union address [January 2011]. He proposed that electric utilities be required to generate 80 percent of their power from clean sources—including renewable energy, energy efficiency, nuclear power, and natural gas—by 2035. The Center for American Progress [a progressive think tank] immediately offered a similar, but more detailed, proposal: one that is guaranteed to generate demand for renewable technologies such as wind and solar power by including a provision requiring that 35 percent of the CES be met by renewable technologies and energy efficiency.

The Senate Energy and Natural Resources Committee is exploring proposals to craft a strong and effective CES. Committee chair Jeff Bingaman (D-NM) and Ranking Republican Lisa Murkowski (R-AK) recently released a white paper seeking comment on a wide range of questions about how to design the most effective CES for the nation. The questions were designed to engage advocates and industry in the initial design of this policy and to show the committee's strong interest in developing a standard that actually works for a variety of regions and industries across the nation.

The Center for American Progress was pleased to respond to the white paper and share our proposal for a CES designed to put the United States on a path toward clean energy leadership. Our responses were guided by proposals that we have developed over the previous year as well as principles that we feel are central to any clean energy policy development.

We believe that for a clean energy standard to be successful it must meet the following core principles:

- Generate new, long-lasting jobs and grow the economy

- Effectively spur development, production, and deployment of renewable energy and energy efficient technologies

- Account for regional diversity in resources and electricity markets

- Be simple and transparent, and minimize costs

- Provide a floor, not a ceiling, for clean energy, strengthening and building on existing state leadership

We commend the committee on its approach to the policy design process and are excited about the prospects for this policy moving forward. The Senate has the opportunity to develop a no-cost, high-impact policy tool that will jumpstart the transformation to a clean energy economy. We hope they will seize that opportunity and provide a key catalyst to move America toward climate stability, energy security, and sustainable economic growth.

Small-Scale Agriculture Is the Key to a Sustainable Future

Peopleandplanet.net

Peopleandplanet.net is a website published by the nonprofit British charity Planet 21. It focuses on issues of population, poverty, health, consumption, and the environment.

Investment in small-scale agriculture, along with more careful use of water, has been emerging, in recent times, as one of the central keys to a sustainable future. Now the influential [environmental group] WorldWatch Institute has endorsed this view with a major report timed to coincide with Earth Day on April 22 [2011].

"Rising temperatures, erratic weather, population growth, and scarce water resources—along with growing civil unrest and skyrocketing food prices—are putting unprecedented stress on people and the planet" it says. But agriculture—often blamed as a driver of environmental problems—is an emerging solution.

"Agriculture is a source of food and income for the world's poor and a primary engine for economic growth. It also offers untapped potential for mitigating climate change and protecting biodiversity, and for lifting millions of people out of poverty."

The report, *Nourishing the Planet*, a two-year evaluation of innovations in agriculture, offers 15 sustainable solutions that are working on the ground to alleviate global hunger while also protecting soil, water, and other vital natural resources. "Agriculture encompasses such a large chunk of the planet that creating healthy economies, mitigating climate change, and improving livelihoods will require a longstanding commitment to the world's farmers," says Danielle Nierenberg, Nourishing the Planet co-project director.

Boosting Soil Fertility

Past attempts to combat hunger have tended to focus narrowly on a few types of crops, rely heavily on chemical fertilizers, and ignore women farmers. "There's been relatively little focus on low-cost ways to boost soil fertility and make better use of scarce water, and on solutions that exist beyond the farm and all along the food chain," says Worldwatch President Christopher Flavin. From urban farming projects that are feeding our growing cities to rotational farming practices that store carbon in the soils and help mitigate climate change, small-scale and low-input innovations can go a long way in protecting the environment—not only on Earth Day, but every day.

From urban farming projects that are feeding our growing cities to rotational farming practices that store carbon in the soils ..., small-scale and low-input innovations can go a long way in protecting the environment.

Sustainable Solutions

The 15 solutions "to guide farmers, scientists, politicians, agribusinesses and aid agencies as they commit to promoting a healthier environment and a more food-secure future" are summarized here: ...

1. *Guaranteeing the Right to Food.* Guaranteeing the human right to adequate food—now and for future generations—requires that policymakers incorporate this right into food security laws and programs at the regional, national, and international level. Governments have a role in providing the public goods to support sustainable agriculture, including ex-

tension services, farmer-to-farmer transmission of knowledge, storage facilities, and infrastructure that links farmers to consumers.

2. Harnessing the Nutritional and Economic Potential of Vegetables. Micronutrient deficiencies, including lack of vitamin A, iodine, and iron, affect 1 billion people worldwide. Promoting indigenous vegetables that are rich in micronutrients could help reduce malnutrition. Locally adapted vegetable varieties are hardier and more dependable than staple crops, making them ideal for smallholder farmers. Research organizations like AVRDC/The World Vegetable Center are developing improved vegetable varieties, such as amaranth and African eggplant, and cultivating an appreciation for traditional foods among consumers.

3. Reducing Food Waste. Experts continue to emphasize increasing global food production, yet our money could be better spent on reducing food waste and post-harvest losses. Already, a number of low-input and regionally appropriate storage and preservation techniques are working to combat food waste around the world. In Pakistan, farmers cut their harvest losses by 70 percent by switching from jute bags and containers constructed with mud to more durable metal containers. And in West Africa, farmers have saved around 100,000 mangos by using solar dryers to dry the fruit after harvest.

4. Feeding Cities. The U.N. [United Nations] estimates that 70 percent of the world's people will live in cities by 2050, putting stress on available food. Urban agriculture projects are helping to improve food security, raise incomes, empower women, and improve urban environments. In sub-Saharan Africa, the Educational Concerns for Hunger Organization (ECHO) has helped city farmers build food gardens, using old tires to create crop beds. And community supported agriculture (CSA) programs in Cape Town, South Africa, are helping to raise incomes and provide produce for school meals.

5. *Getting More Crop per Drop.* Many small farmers lack access to a reliable source of water, and water supplies are drying up as extraction exceeds sustainable levels. Only 4 percent of sub-Saharan Africa's cultivated land is equipped for irrigation, and a majority of households depend on rainfall to water their crops, which climate scientists predict will decline in coming decades. Efficient water management in agriculture can boost crop productivity for these farmers. By practicing conservation tillage, weeding regularly, and constructing vegetative barriers and earthen dams, farmers can harness rainfall more effectively.

Agricultural practices, such as agroforestry and the regeneration of natural resources, can help mitigate climate change.

---

6. *Using Farmers' Knowledge in Research and Development.* Agricultural research and development processes typically exclude smallholder farmers and their wealth of knowledge, leading to less-efficient agricultural technologies that go unused. Research efforts that involve smallholder farmers alongside agricultural scientists can help meet specific local needs, strengthen farmers' leadership abilities, and improve how research and education systems operate. In southern Ethiopia's Amaro district, a community-led body carried out an evaluation of key problems and promising solutions using democratic decision-making to determine what type of research should be funded.

7. *Improving Soil Fertility.* Africa's declining soil fertility may lead to an imminent famine; already, it is causing harvest productivity to decline 15–25 percent, and farmers expect harvests to drop by half in the next five years. Green manure/cover crops, including living trees, bushes, and vines, help restore soil quality and are an inexpensive and feasible solution to this problem. In the drought-prone Sahel region, the Dogon

people of Mali are using an innovative, three-tiered system and are now harvesting three times the yield achieved in other parts of the Sahel.

8. *Safeguarding Local Food Biodiversity.* Over the past few decades, traditional African agriculture based on local diversity has given way to monoculture crops destined for export. Less-healthy imports are replacing traditional, nutritionally rich foods, devastating local economies and diets. Awareness-raising initiatives and efforts to improve the quality of production and marketing are adding value to and encouraging diversification and consumption of local products. In Ethiopia's Wukro and Wenchi villages, honey producers are training with Italian and Ethiopian beekeepers to process and sell their honey more efficiently, promote appreciation for local food, and compete with imported products.

9. *Coping with Climate Change and Building Resilience.* Global climate change, including higher temperatures and increased periods of drought, will negatively impact agriculture by reducing soil fertility and decreasing crop yields. Although agriculture is a major contributor to climate change, accounting for about one-third of global emissions, agricultural practices, such as agroforestry and the re-generation of natural resources, can help mitigate climate change. In Niger, farmers have planted nearly 5 million hectares of trees that conserve water, prevent soil erosion, and sequester carbon, making their farms more productive and drought-resistant without damaging the environment.

10. *Harnessing the Knowledge and Skills of Women Farmers.* According to the U.N. Food and Agriculture Organization, women represent 43 percent of the agricultural labor force, but due to limited access to inputs, land, and services, they produce less per unit of land than their male counterparts. Improving women's access to agricultural extension services, credit programs, and information technology can help empower women, while reducing global hunger and poverty. In

Uganda, extension programs are introducing women farmers to coolbot technology, which uses solar energy and an inverter to reduce temperatures and prolong the shelf life of vegetables.

11. *Investing in Africa's Land: Crisis and Opportunity.* As pressure to increase food production rises, wealthy countries in the Middle East and Asia are acquiring cheap land in Africa to increase their food productivity. This has led to the exploitation of small-scale African farmers, compromising their food security. Agricultural investment models that create collaborations between African farmers and the foreign investing countries can be part of the solution. In Ethiopia's Rift Valley, farmers grow green beans for the Dutch market during the European winter months, but cultivate corn and other crops for local consumption during the remaining months.

12. *Charting a New Path to Eliminating Hunger.* Nearly 1 billion people around the world are hungry, 239 million of whom live in sub-Saharan Africa. To alleviate hunger, we must shift our attention beyond the handful of crops that have absorbed most of agriculture's attention and focus on ways to improve farmers' access to inputs and make better use of the food already produced. Innovations—such as the human-powered pump that can increase access to irrigation and low-cost plastic bags that help preserve grains—offer models that can be scaled-up and replicated beyond Africa.

13. *Moving Ecoagriculture into the Mainstream.* Agricultural practices that emphasize increased production have contributed to the degradation of land, soil, and local ecosystems, and ultimately hurt the livelihoods of the farmers who depend on these natural resources. Agroecological methods, including organic farming practices, can help farmers protect natural resources and provide a sustainable alternative to costly industrial inputs. These include rotational grazing for livestock in Zimbabwe's Savanna region and tea plantations in Kenya, where farmers use intercropping to improve soil quality and boost yields.

14. *Improving Food Production from Livestock.* In the coming decades, small livestock farmers in the developing world will face unprecedented challenges: demand for animal-source foods, such as milk and meat, is increasing, while animal diseases in tropical countries will continue to rise, hindering trade and putting people at risk. Innovations in livestock feed, disease control, and climate change adaptation—as well as improved yields and efficiency—are improving farmers' incomes and making animal-source food production more sustainable. In India, farmers are improving the quality of their feed by using grass, sorghum, stover, and brans to produce more milk from fewer animals.

15. *Going Beyond Production.* Although scarcity and famine dominate the discussion of food security in sub-Saharan Africa, many countries are unequipped to deal with the crop surpluses that lead to low commodity prices and food waste. Helping farmers better organize their means of production—from ordering inputs to selling their crops to a customer—can help them become more resilient to fluctuations in global food prices and better serve local communities that need food. In Uganda, the organization TechnoServe has helped to improve market conditions for banana farmers by forming business groups through which they can buy inputs, receive technical advice, and sell their crops collectively.

Researchers with Nourishing the Planet travelled to 25 countries across sub-Saharan Africa, where they met with over 250 farmers' groups, scientists, NGOs [non-governmental organizations], and government agencies. WorldWatch says their stories of hope and success serve as models for large-scale efforts beyond Africa. The project's recently-released *State of the World 2011: Innovations that Nourish the Planet* report draws from over 60 of the world's leading agricultural experts and provides a roadmap for the funding and donor communities.

Asian Countries Must Reduce Black Carbon Air Pollution Emissions

Neeno Pandora

Neeno Pandora is a photographer and writer currently studying at the London College of Communication in the United Kingdom.

Once you have visited China you realise the real reason why so many of Asians wear those face masks. It's not for subtle medical purposes. It's to escape suffocating from pollution. I have been here a day and am finding it hard to breathe. You could call it smog or haze: I call it the ABC. The Asian Brown Cloud.

The air pollution from cooking fires, coal fired power plants, and gasoline and diesel engines is the cause. This air pollution is measurable across the Pacific and into the West Coast of the U.S. Air pollution (from different areas of the world) has its own unique signature. A recent study indicated that about 30% of San Francisco's particulate levels are from China.

China's Smog and Haze

Smog frequently builds up in eastern China during the winter when weather conditions trap pollutants over the plain. Haze had been reported over Beijing for much of the previous week [April 11, 2011]. . . .

[China's haze] contains mostly soot or black carbon, and possibly some ground-level ozone. Soot is released from burning fossil fuels (particularly diesel and coal), wood, and other biofuels. These same processes also release chemicals that

Neeno Pandora, "China's Air Pollution: The Need for Solutions," *Urban Times*, April 18, 2011. Used by permission.

combine in sunlight to form ozone: methane, nitrogen oxides, volatile organic compounds, and carbon monoxide. In China, coal is an important fuel burned in home heating and cooking and energy production.

Asian countries, particularly China and India, emit the most soot in the world, and would therefore see the greatest economic and health benefits in reducing emissions.

Both soot and ozone cause respiratory problems and can permanently damage the lungs. Ozone harms plants, which decreases food production. Soot and methane (one of the gases that create ozone) also contribute to global warming. In fact, a UN [United Nations] report to be released this week found that reducing emissions of black carbon and methane would cut global warming in half over the next forty years. By cutting carbon dioxide emissions as well as controlling soot and methane, the global temperature change could be kept under 2 degrees Celsius (4 degrees Fahrenheit) in the short term.

The panel of 70 scientists that prepared the report for the United Nations Environment Program identified 16 control measures, such as installing clean-burning cooking stoves and putting particle filters on vehicles, that would significantly reduce black carbon and methane pollution using existing technologies. The measures would also improve air quality and increase food production, preventing as many as 2.5 million deaths.

Asian countries, particularly China and India, emit the most soot in the world, and would therefore see the greatest economic and health benefits in reducing emissions. To read more, see "Cleaning the Air Would Limit Short-term Climate Warming", an interview with Drew Shindell, the NASA [National Aeronautics and Space Administration] climatologist who led the scientific panel.

NASA tracks pollution worldwide using a variety of sensors, including MODIS [Moderate Resolution Imaging Spectroradiometer]. However, the most valuable sensor for monitoring soot is the NASA satellite, Glory, which launched on February 23, 2011. Glory is able to differentiate between different types of particles in the atmosphere to monitor the impact of man-made particles, like soot, on Earth's climate.

Let's hope we find a solution to pollution before it is too late.

China Must Improve Its Environmental Protections

Wang Jin

Wang Jin is a professor at Peking University in China and an expert in environmental law.

Since 1979, the National People's Congress [of China] and its Standing Committee have passed as many as 280 pieces of legislation, of which 29—almost 10%—relate to environmental resources, energy and clean production. No one can say that legislative efforts in this field have been weak. In addition, civil, criminal and business laws have grown to include regulation on environmental and resource protection, subjects that have also featured in the rulings of the State Council, China's highest administrative authority.

Similarly, environmental-protection bodies have developed and expanded and their powers strengthened. The number of environmental-protection personnel employed at all levels of government has increased annually, an environmental law enforcement system is under construction and the number of monitoring bodies is constantly increasing.

At the same time, the government's own figures on the state of the environment show that air and water pollution in China have already reached a critical level. Official data indicates that 150 million mu [10,000 square kilometres] of arable land in China—one tenth of our total—has been affected by pollution. Rates of cancer and other diseases are increasing, and the number of disputes over pollution has increased by 20% to 25% every year since 1996.

Problems with China's Environmental Laws

Clearly, there are major problems with the implementation of China's environmental laws. In most western countries, legis-

Wang Jin, "China's Green Laws Are Useless," *China Dialogue*, September 23, 2010. Used by permission of China Dialogue.

lation is evaluated some time after implementation. If China were to do the same, I believe we would find our environmental laws have failed. There are several key issues behind this:

First, China's whole legal system is not working well because the nation's basic legislative system is incomplete. For example, the Property Law of the People's Republic of China, which came into force as late as 2007, and the Tort Law, which was only enacted last year, not to mention a number of regulations that make up the country's administrative laws—governing organisations, procedures and enforcement—are still filled with holes. Moreover, criminal law as regards pollution is extremely weak: as long as no major pollution of the environment, no major loss of property and no major injuries result, then there is no crime. And those who pollute in the full knowledge that they are putting public health at risk are not classed as criminals.

Second, although there were no major errors in the drafting of the environmental laws, it did not produce legislation of any great merit either. In China, when you want to apply the law in order to enforce some particular responsibility, more often than not you find there is no applicable regulation.

Third, the actual articles of the law and the law's overall aims often contradict each other. For example, there are limits on the release of pollution, but businesses are allowed to exceed those limits if they pay a fee. In spite of the law being tightened, such breaches happen all the time, and in order to collect the ensuing fines—and thereby fulfil this aspect of their duties—environmental-protection officials allow the situation to continue.

Similar Problems with China's Environmental Assessment System

We see the same thing with the environmental-impact assessment (EIA) system. The law stresses the importance of prevention, but allows a company to go ahead with a project even if it has not carried out an assessment—as long as it promises to do one further down the line. According to our research, across the country, more than 50% of EIAs are dealt with in this way. High polluting and energy-consuming firms, in particular, are fans of this approach; if they have already got the local licence and other relevant permissions for a project, they can force through approval of their EIA, but if they talk about the EIA in advance, it's highly likely that it won't go through.

Similar problems are found in the realms of public participation, open information, the implementation of rectification orders and on-site checks. The truth is that all of China's laws are like this: on the surface, they look great, but when it comes to implementation, they are useless.

In May 2010, the government of Guzhen county, in the eastern province of Anhui, removed six local environmental-protection officials—including the bureau chief—from their posts. They had checked up on one firm three times within a 20 day period, a move the government claimed was damaging efforts to attract investment. A local Anhui province law requires environmental authorities to obtain approval before making checks. Other places are following suit, with the result that the biggest polluters and energy consumers are being protected by local government.

Implementation Difficulties

Implementation of environmental law is also affected by several judicial factors:

First, there are difficulties enforcing the sanctions handed out to polluting firms. If the company does not comply with the ruling, an application for court enforcement can be made—but the courts are unenthusiastic about this measure. In many areas, courts are graded on successful implementation of their own judgements in lawsuits. These administrative environmental punishments do not arise from their lawsuits, and therefore enforcing them does not increase the rating of the court.

Second, even getting to the point where a lawsuit is heard is tough, as courts can refuse to accept cases. China's supreme court and local courts have regulations on the handling of so-called sensitive or special cases, meaning they can refuse to let someone bring an action and leave them with no other options to pursue. A survey of 12,000 judicial employees I once carried out found that 50% believed lawsuits were regularly being refused by courts in the name of social stability.

[Third], if the case is accepted, it may not be heard. If it is heard, a judgement may not be given. And if there is a judgement, it may not be enforced.

[Fourth], it is rare that criminal responsibility for pollution is enforced—while those who use violence to protest pollution are often prosecuted. There are so many cases where victims who have had enough of constant pollution breaches and have no means open to them of bringing a lawsuit, are finally forced to resort to violence in order to fight the polluters.

Laws without regulation, troops without power, duties without action: in the final assessment, this is the current state of environmental law in China.

Some time back, a lawyer from the All-China Lawyers Association's Environmental and Resources Law Committee was representing a man who, driven to his wits end, had taken direct action against a firm in the interests of self-protection. He was subsequently arrested and charged with disrupting production. In court, the lawyer said: "Companies that continuously break pollution regulations are carrying out illegal production. Local governments and the courts should pursue them in accordance with the law." The court held that illegal pollution did not constitute illegal production—but that it was against the law to cut off the company's power or block its roads.

Other Flaws

China's environmental standards can also, inadvertently, cause harm. China currently has 20 standards for atmospheric pollution, compared to 187 in the United States. So during the 2008 Olympics, when reporters complained about Beijing's poor air quality, China proudly retorted that it had met its standards. How could this be? China does not, for example, have a standard for particulate matter of 2.5 nanometres or less—and if you don't have a standard, you can't breach it. This is an obvious flaw.

In addition to all of the above, there are also problems with the quantity and quality of available personnel and inadequate technology. Meanwhile, the actual amount of money spent on pollution control is far less than the authorities claim—we have seen this reflected in many individual cases, where it is claimed that hundreds of millions of yuan has been spent, but the real investment is much lower. This issue is related to insufficient funding for environmental protection.

Laws without regulation, troops without power, duties without action: in the final assessment, this is the current state of environmental law in China.

Combating Pollution Requires International Solutions

VOAnews.com

VOAnews.com is a website run by the Voice Of America, a radio and television broadcasting service of the US federal government that provides news and entertainment programs throughout the world in an effort to promote understanding of US culture and policies.

"Pollution doesn't stop at international borders, and neither can our environmental and health protections," said U.S. Environmental Protection Agency [EPA] Administrator Lisa Jackson. At a meeting in Guanajuato, Mexico, of the Commission for Environmental Cooperation, August 17th [2010], Administrator Jackson announced 6 international priorities that will guide U.S. environmental protection policy in months and years ahead.

US International Priorities for Environmental Protection

The priorities include building strong environmental institutions and legal structures. EPA will work in partnership with countries such as Ghana, Kenya and Brazil to support the promotion of good governance, improve judicial and legal structures and advise on the design of regulatory systems necessary for effective environmental protection around the world.

Combating climate change by limiting pollution is another priority. EPA has taken important steps to reduce greenhouse gas emissions in the United States, but the global challenge of climate change requires a global solution. EPA will promote global strategies to reduce greenhouse gas emissions such as methane from industry and agriculture and other pollutants

"Pollution—A Global Threat," VOAnews.com, September 8, 2010.

such as black carbon from cook stoves. These pollutants are damaging especially vulnerable regions such as the Himalayan glaciers and the Arctic.

The United States is committed to working with the international community to meet [environmental] challenges.

Improving air and water quality are also important goals. Asthma and other respiratory illnesses are increasing due to air pollution worldwide. EPA will work with organizations and countries such as Indonesia to improve urban air quality in developing cities and communities. EPA will support global partners and regions, such as the Caribbean in creating safe and efficient drinking water and wastewater treatment systems. The agency will also help in providing long-term, sustainable and high-quality drinking water and sanitation systems for overburdened and underserved communities such as those along the U.S.-Mexico border.

Chemicals are prevalent in everything from food to baby bottles. As children develop, they are especially vulnerable to these chemicals, particularly mercury and lead. EPA will work closely with global partners to provide protections for people and consistency for industry. Working with partners such as the United Nations Environmental Programme, EPA will strive to reduce or eliminate the impact of pesticides and other toxic chemicals on human health and the environment.

The electronics that provide us with convenience often end up discarded in developing countries where improper disposal can threaten local people and the environment. EPA recognizes this important concern and will work with international partners to address the issues of E-waste in the near term.

"Our challenges are shared challenges," said EPA Administrator Jackson. The United States is committed to working with the international community to meet those challenges.

Organizations to Contact

The editors have compiled the following list of organizations concerned with the issues debated in this book. The descriptions are derived from materials provided by the organizations. All have publications or information available for interested readers. The list was compiled on the date of publication of the present volume; names, addresses, phone and fax numbers, and e-mail and Internet addresses may change. Be aware that many organizations take several weeks or longer to respond to inquiries, so allow as much time as possible.

American Lung Association (ALA)
1301 Pennsylvania Ave. NW, Suite 800
Washington, DC   20004
(202) 785-3355 • fax: (202) 452-1805
e-mail: info@lungusa.org
website: www.lungusa.org

Founded in 1904 to fight tuberculosis, the American Lung Association currently fights lung disease in all its forms, with special emphasis on asthma, tobacco control, and environmental health. The ALA website is a source of articles, fact sheets, and special reports on pollution-related issues, including its yearly "State of the Air" report, which analyzes improvements or deterioration of air quality in the United States.

Cato Institute
1000 Massachusetts Ave. NW, Washington, DC   20001-5403
(202) 842-0200 • fax: (202) 842-3490
e-mail: cato@cato.org
website: www.cato.org

The Cato Institute is a libertarian public policy research organization dedicated to limiting the role of government and protecting individual liberties. The institute publishes the quarterly magazine, *Regulation*, and the bimonthly *Cato Policy*

Report. Its website contains a research topic called "Energy and Environment" that provides links to a wealth of Cato publications dealing with energy, global warming, pollution, environmental regulation, natural resources, and urban growth and transportation. Cato's energy and environment work is focused on promoting policies that allow the free markets, rather than government, to decide questions about environmental standards. Examples of publications include "Harsh Climate for Trade: How Climate Change Proposals Threaten Global Commerce" and "Scientific Misconduct: The Manipulation of Evidence for Political Advocacy in Health Care and Climate Policy."

Competitive Enterprise Institute (CEI)
1899 L St. NW, Floor 12, Washington, DC   20036
(202) 331-1010 • fax: (202) 331-0640
e-mail: info@cei.org
website: www.cei.org

CEI is a public policy organization dedicated to the principles of free enterprise and limited government. The institute supports market-based pollution policies. On its website, CEI publishes books, articles, editorials, speeches, studies, and op-eds. Examples of recent op-eds include "The Price of Beauty: Chemicals in My Cosmetics?" and "Oregon's Anti-BPA Packaging Legislation May Jeopardize Public Health."

Earth Island Institute (EII)
2150 Allston Way, Suite 460, Berkeley, CA   94704-1375
(510) 859-9100 • fax: (510) 859-9091
website: www.earthisland.org

Founded in 1982 by veteran environmentalist David Brower, Earth Island Institute is a nonprofit, public interest, membership organization that promotes the conservation, preservation, and restoration of the environment. EII publishes the quarterly *Earth Island Journal.* Recent journal articles include "Yellowstone Oil Spill Highlights Need for Better Safety Rules" and "Breaking Down Bioplastics: Is the Bioplastic Cup Half Full or Half Empty?"

Earth Policy Institute (EPI)
1350 Connecticut Ave. NW, Suite 403, Washington, DC   20036
(202) 496-9290 • fax: (202) 496-9325
e-mail: epi@earthpolicy.org
website: www.earth-policy.org

The Earth Policy Institute is an organization founded in 2001 by Lester Brown, the founder and former president of the Worldwatch Institute, to promote a sustainable future. EPI works at the global level to provide a global plan for moving the world onto an environmentally and economically sustainable path and to engage the media, academics, and policymakers in this effort. The group's website is a source of numerous publications, including books, updates, and other information. Recent updates include "Geothermal Power Heating Up Worldwide," "When the Nile Runs Dry," and "Cancer Now Leading Cause of Death in China."

Environmental Protection Agency (EPA)
Ariel Rios Bldg., 1200 Pennsylvania Ave. NW
Washington, DC   20460
(202) 272-0167
website: www.epa.gov

The Environmental Protection Agency is the US federal agency in charge of protecting the environment and controlling pollution. The agency works toward these goals by assisting businesses and local environmental agencies, enacting and enforcing regulations, identifying and fining polluters, and cleaning up polluted sites. On its website, the EPA has links to specific pollution issues, including air and water pollution, climate change, green living, and pesticides, chemicals, and toxics. The EPA website is a great source for information on a wide variety of pollution-related topics. Among the resources available are recent reports and publications such as "Inventory of US Greenhouse Gas Emissions and Sinks: 1990–2009" and "Climate Change Science Facts."

Friends of the Earth (FOE)
1100 15th St. NW, Floor 11, Washington, DC   20005
(877) 843-8687
website: www.foe.org

Friends of the Earth is a progressive environmental organization that seeks to defend the environment and create a more healthy and just world. It is part of Friends of the Earth International, a federation of grassroots environmental groups working in seventy-six countries. The group's current focus is on promoting clean energy and solutions to climate change, keeping toxins out of food and consumer products, and protecting marine ecosystems. The FOE website contains useful news and updates on a variety of topics, including global warming, air and water pollution, and clean energy, and publishes a quarterly *Friends of the Earth Newsmagazine*. The spring 2011 edition of this magazine contains such articles as "Eliminating Taxpayer Giveaways to Polluters" and "Radioactive Energy: The Prospects for Nuclear in the Wake of Fukushima."

Greenpeace
702 H St. NW, Washington, DC   20001
(800) 722-6995
e-mail: info@wdc.greenpeace.org
website: www.greenpeace.org

Greenpeace is a private membership organization of environmental activists with offices in more than forty countries. It stages peaceful protests and other activities to expose global environmental problems, such as ocean pollution, global warming, and deforestation. The group publishes blogs, press releases, and updates on environmental issues. Recent publications include, for example, "Coal Lobby Fails, Healthier Air in Sight" and "Germany Sets the Bar for a Green Energy Future."

Heritage Foundation
214 Massachusetts Ave. NE, Washington, DC   20002-4999
(800) 546-4400 • fax: (202) 546-8328

e-mail: info@heritage.org
website: www.heritage.org

The Heritage Foundation is a conservative think tank that supports free enterprise and limited government. Its researchers often criticize environmental over-regulation and oppose government subsidies to promote clean energy. It publishes a quarterly magazine, *Policy Review*, as well as numerous articles and commentaries. Recent Heritage articles include "American Energy Freedom: The Basis for Economic Recovery" and "Obama's Radical Climate Change Agenda Driving US Foreign Aid Policy."

Natural Resources Defense Council (NRDC)
40 W 20th St., New York, NY   10011
(212) 727-2700 • fax: (212)727-1773
website: www.nrdc.org

The Natural Resources Defense Council is a nonprofit organization that uses law, science, and more than four hundred thousand members nationwide to protect the planet's wildlife and wild places and to ensure a safe and healthy environment for all living things. NRDC publishes *Nature's Voice*, a bimonthly bulletin of environmental news, and *OnEarth*, an environmental magazine. Its website also provides a wealth of information about specific pollution-related topics, such as global warming, clean energy, oceans, air, and water. Publications include fact sheets, reports, news, and articles, including such reports as "The New Energy Economy: Putting America on the Path to Solving Global Warming" and "Drilling Down: Protecting Western Communities from the Health and Environmental Effects of Oil and Gas Production."

Pew Charitable Trusts
901 E St. NW, Washington, DC   20004-2008
(202) 552-2000 • fax: (202) 552-2299
website: www.pewtrusts.org

The Pew Charitble Trusts is an independent nonprofit organization that is funded by seven individual charitable funds established between 1948 and 1979 by two sons and two daughters of Sun Oil Company founder Joseph N. Pew and his wife, Mary Anderson Pew. The organization studies and promotes nonpartisan solutions for national and global public policy problems, using impartial, fact-based, public-opinion polling and other research tools to track important issues and trends. The group's issues include the environment, which is the focus of the Pew Environment Group (www.pewenvironment.org). This part of the Pew Trusts seeks to protect ocean and land habitats and advocates for a clean energy economy, and it offers a wealth of news, research, and information. Recent publications include, for example, "Industrial Animal Agriculture Is Not a Pretty Picture," "Driving Toward Energy Independence," and "Overfishing 101: The Importance of Rebuilding Our Fish Populations Without Delay."

Physicians for Social Responsibility (PSR)
1875 Connecticut Ave. NW, Suite 1012
Washington, DC   20009
(202) 667-4260 • fax: (202) 667-4201
website: www.psr.org

Founded in 1961, Physicians for Social Responsibility is a nonprofit organization that works to prevent nuclear war and proliferation and to slow, stop, and reverse global warming and toxic degradation of the environment. PSR's mission is to protect human life from these threats. The PSR website contains a program that focuses mainly on environmental toxins and global warming. It is also a source of information, including reports such as "The Clean Air Act: A Proven Tool for Healthy Air" and "Coal Ash: The Toxic Threat to Our Health and Environment."

Union of Concerned Scientists (UCS)
2 Brattle Square, Cambridge, MA   02238-9105
(617) 547-5552 • fax: (617) 864-9405
website: www.ucsusa.org

The Union of Concerned Scientists is a science-based nonprofit advocacy group that works for a healthy environment and a safer world. UCS publishes a biannual magazine, *Cata-*

lyst, as well as a quarterly newsletter, *Earthwise*, a monthly list of environmental tips called *Green Tips*, and a variety of books and reports. Its website also contains valuable information about global warming and other environmental topics. Examples of recent publications include "Climate 2030: A National Blueprint for a Clean Energy Economy" and "The Consumer's Guide to Effective Environmental Choices: Practical Advice from the Union of Concerned Scientists."

Worldwatch Institute
1776 Massachusetts Ave. NW, Washington, DC   20036-1904
(202) 452-1999
website: www.worldwatch.org

Worldwatch is a nonprofit public policy research organization dedicated to informing policymakers and the public about emerging global problems and trends and the complex links between the world economy and its environmental support systems. It publishes the bimonthly *World Watch* magazine, an annual "State of the World" report, various policy papers, and other news items, articles, and blogs. Recent and archived issues of *World Watch* are available on its website, as well as such publications as "State of the World 2011: Innovations that Nourish the Planet," "Nuclear Power After Fukushima," and "Population, Climate Change, and Women's Lives."

Bibliography

Books

Committee on the Significance of International Transport of Air Pollutants and National Research Council
Global Sources of Local Pollution: An Assessment of Long-Range Transport of Key Air Pollutants to and from the United States. Washington, DC: National Academies Press, 2010.

C. David Cooper and F.C. Alley
Air Pollution Control: A Design Approach. Long Grove, IL: Waveland Press, 2010.

Douglas Cormack
Response to Marine Oil Pollution: Review and Assessment. New York: Springer, 2010.

Dietrich Earnhart and Robert Glicksman
Pollution Limits and Polluters' Efforts to Comply: The Role of Government Monitoring and Enforcement. Palo Alto, CA: Stanford Economics and Finance, 2011.

Kevin Christopher Elliott
Is a Little Pollution Good for You?: Incorporating Societal Values in Environmental Research. New York: Oxford University Press, 2011.

Bhola R. Gurjar, Luisa T. Molina, and C.S.P. Ojha
Air Pollution: Health and Environmental Impacts. Boca Raton, FL: CRC Press, 2010.

Marquita K. Hill
Understanding Environmental Pollution. Cambridge, MA: Cambridge University Press, 2010.

David Kirby   *Animal Factory: The Looming Threat of Industrial Pig, Dairy, and Poultry Farms to Humans and the Environment.* New York: St. Martin's Press, 2010.

Lester B. Lave and   *Air Pollution and Human Health.* Eugene P. Seskin   Oxford, United Kingdom: RFF Press, 2011.

Ibrahim A. Mirsal   *Soil Pollution: Origin, Monitoring & Remediation.* New York: Springer, 2010.

A. Ed El Nemr   *Environmental Pollution and Its Relation to Climate Change.* Hauppauge, NY: Nova Science Publishers, Inc., 2011.

Robert F. Phalen   *Introduction to Air Pollution Science.* and Robert N.   Sudbury, MA: Jones & Bartlett Phalen   Learning, 2011.

Arnold W. Reitze   *Air Pollution Control and Climate Change Mitigation Law, Second Ed.* Washington, DC: Environmental Law Institute, 2010.

Marie-Monique   *The World According to Monsanto:* Robin   *Pollution, Corruption, and the Control of the World's Food Supply.* New York: New Press, 2010.

Francis A. Schaeffer, Udo W. Middelmann, Lynn White Jr., and Richard Means
Pollution and the Death of Man. Wheaton, IL: Crossway Books, 2011.

Michel Serres and Anne-Marie Feenberg-Dibon
Malfeasance: Appropriation Through Pollution? Palo Alto, CA: Stanford University Press, 2010.

N. H. Stern
The Global Deal: Climate Change and the Creation of a New Era of Progress and Prosperity. New York: PublicAffairs, 2009

US Government, Environmental Protection Agency, Department of Energy, and US Geological Survey
21st Century Guide to Hydraulic Fracturing, Underground Injection, Fracking, Hydrofrac, Marcellus Shale Natural Gas Production Controversy, Environmental and Safety Risks, Water Pollution (CD-ROM). Chula Vista, CA: Progressive Management, 2010.

Horatio R. Velasquez
Pollution Control: Management, Technology and Regulations. Hauppauge, NY: Nova Science Publishers, 2011.

Philip Wexler, Jan van der Kolk, Asish Mohapatra, and Ravi Agarwal
Chemicals, Environment, Health: A Global Management Perspective. Boca Raton, FL: CRC Press, 2011.

Periodicals and Internet Sources

Jonathan Ansfield and Keith Bradsher	"China Report Shows More Pollution in Waterways," *New York Times*, February 9, 2010. www.nytimes.com.
Associated Press	"Biologist: Ocean Pollution 'Threatening the Human Food Supply,'" *Raw Story*, June 24, 2010. www.rawstory.com.
David Biello	"Ocean Impact Map Reveals Human Reach Global," *Scientific American*, February 15, 2008. www.scientific american.com.
Bettina Boxall and Alana Semuels	"Signs of Oil Spill Pollution Might Be Hiding Underwater," *Los Angeles Times*, May 16, 2010. http://articles .latimes.com.
Elena Craft	"Five Air Pollution Stories You Might Have Missed in 2010," Environmental Defense Fund, December 30, 2010. http://blogs.edf.org.
Travis Donovan	"State of the Ocean: 'Shocking' Report Warns of Mass Extinction from Current Rate of Marine Distress," *Huffington Post*, June 20, 2011. www.huffingtonpost.com.
Environmental Leader	"93% View Water Pollution as 'Serious' Problem," August 18, 2009. www.environmentalleader.com.

Alex Frangos — "An Overhead View of China's Pollution," *Wall Street Journal*, September 27, 2010. http://blogs.wsj.com.

Daniel G. Huber and Jay Gulledge — "Extreme Weather and Climate Change: Understanding the Link, Managing the Risk," Pew Center on Global Climate Change, June 2011. www.pewclimate.org.

Andrew Jacobs — "In China, Pollution Worsens Despite New Efforts," *New York Times*, July 28, 2010. www.nytimes.com.

Brad Johnson — "EPA Will Begin Regulating Industrial Global Warming Pollution in March 2010," *Think Progress*, September 30, 2009. http://thinkprogress.org.

Leslie Kaufman — "Scientists' Report Stresses Urgency of Limiting Greenhouse Gas Emissions," *New York Times*, May 12, 2011. www.nytimes.com.

Josh Ketchen — "Global Warming Equals Political, Real World Equals Cooling," *WeatherTech*, May 15, 2011. www.myweathertech.com.

Gene J. Koprowski — "Al Gore Explains 'Snowmageddon,'" FoxNews.com, February 3, 2011. www.foxnews.com.

Bruce McQuain   "Former 'Alarmist' Scientist Says Anthropogenic Global Warming (AGW) Based in False Science," *Hot Air*, May 15, 2011. http://hotair.com.

New York Times   "Global Warming," July 1, 2011. http://topics.nytimes.com.

J. Timmons Roberts, Bradley C. Parks, Michael J. Tierney, and Robert L. Hicks   "Has Foreign Aid Been Greened?" *Environment*, January–February 2009. www.environmentmagazine.org.

Rodale   "Everything You Do Makes a Difference: How Ocean and Human Health Connect," April 6, 2011. www.rodale.com.

Scientific American   "Is Global Warming a Myth? How to Respond to People Who Doubt the Human Impact on the Climate," April 8, 2009. www.scientific american.com.

David Stanway   "Water, CO_2 the Priorities for China's 5-Year Plan," *Planet Ark*, March 4, 2011. http://planetark.org.

Mark Tapscott   "Obama Pouring Billions into Global Warming at EPA Despite Growing Evidence of Fraudulent Data," *Washington Examiner*, February 2, 2010. http://washington examiner.com.

Daniel J. Weiss and Kate Gordon — "Pollution Limits Are Essential for Clean Energy Investments: 'Energy Only' Bills Short Change New Technologies," Center for American Progress, March 30, 2010. www.americanprogress.org.

Lijin Zhong and Cy Jones — "China Needs Comprehensive and Cost-effective Strategies to Address Water Pollution," *The Water Project: China*, 2011. www.asiawater project.org.

Index